~~UN~~-LOVED:

The Life and Stories of Arthur Seftel

WRITTEN AND EDITED BY

Lisa DellaVecchia

UN-LOVED: The Life and Stories of Arthur Seftel

Written and Edited by Lisa DellaVecchia

The Jeremiad Christian Homesteaders Gazette, Publisher
www.jeremiadchristianhomesteadersgazette.com

©2023 by Lisa DellaVecchia. All rights reserved.

Printed in the United States of America.

ISBN: 979-8-9889300-5-1

5 4 3 2 1

Preface

It's Friday, November 3, 2023, and I'm finally sitting down to put the finishing touches on this wonderful collection of phone interviews that I conducted with my grandfather, Arthur Seftel, between December 2022 and April 2023. He was 94 at the time of these interviews.

This book is organized into chapters, and the order of the chapters and the ideas contained within them very roughly correspond to the chronology of phone interviews (15 to 20 of them) over this time period. I took the liberty of moving some things around when it made sense to do so, and I filled in some gaps in information over the months between April and now over several more conversations.

Some of the ideas are so interrelated that they necessarily needed to loop back from a later period into an earlier period and then back again. Any repetition you may find is intentional, as each memory builds on itself in order to tell the complete story, and to relate it to different things in different ways.

Everything you will read in the ensuing chapters is a transcription of what Grandpa Artie told me, and I tried to retain his tone and his phraseology exactly as he presented it to me. My goal was this: In your mind's "ear," you should be able to hear *Grandpa Artie* saying these words to you, not me, as you move through the pages of this book—especially if you know him well.

A Note About the Family Names

In no way did I go into the *entire* family tree to tell Grandpa's stories, nor would that have been appropriate or relevant. The main "character" of this story is Grandpa Artie, but Grandma Rita's story is, of course, inextricably linked with his, since they were husband and wife. The stories he tells greatly hinge on their marriage and how close they were, and yet on how different they were. So not every family member is mentioned here, nor could it have been possible to do so.

As a map to navigate the pages of this book, here is the basic outline of names. Grandpa Artie had a mother, a father, and a stepmother. These people are *unnamed* in the story on purpose, and you'll see why as you read the story. He had a half-brother Harry and a brother Sidney. Grandma Rita had two brothers: Theodore and Stuart. Grandma Rita's parents were Grandma Rae and Grandpa Joe. Grandma Rita and Grandpa Artie had two children: Sharon and Teddy. Sharon is my mother; she had me in 1967 and she had my half-sister Janina in 1973. We, in turn, had children of our own.

All references just to "Grandma" are talking about my Grandma Rita, since my grandfather is speaking directly to me in these interviews, and to me, "Grandma" can mean nobody else *but* Grandma Rita. Whenever he says "you" in these pages, he is talking about me.

The point of this book was not to give a detailed genealogy of every single person who ever sprang from Arthur Seftel. The point was to tell *his* story, as he wanted to tell it, and for the reasons he wanted to tell it, and that's what I set out to do here by capturing these interviews and piecing them together.

From Homework Assignment to Book Project

The idea for the book stemmed from my daughter's middle school homework project in early December 2022. The assignment was to interview someone who has been around for a long time and to get their perspective on world events and other things that would place them in that time period. The task was to capture memories all but lost now, as most of the people in Grandpa's generation have passed on, including Grandma. I think it was an excellent assignment, considering that kids today are steeped in a world of technology and sound bites, with no concept at all of what it was like when phones were still attached to walls with a curly vinyl cord and computers didn't exist (me), let alone when horses were still driving fruit carts up and down city streets (Grandpa).

As I was helping to collect as much information as possible for this small assignment, it dawned on Grandpa and me that he actually had a *huge* story to tell—and almost a *burden* on his heart to tell it. We both agreed that I would be his scribe and he would tell his entire life story to me. And I promised him I'd make it into a book.

For the Someones and Everyone

It doesn't ultimately matter how many people will or will not end up reading this book cover to cover. What matters most is that Grandpa's story is told, and that all of these memories are not lost to history. The ones who love him—and there are *so, so* many—will definitely find this book to be a treasure. For those who have never had the pleasure of knowing him, there are perspectives here that no sociology textbook or website could ever give you. Though the stories are personal and specific, the struggles behind these stories reveal universal truths and a way of looking at life that could really benefit someone. In fact, that was one of the big motivations behind my grandfather's commitment to this book—it was definitely to help someone, or as he put it, the "someones" who are out there, wherever they may be. Another motivation, as I perceived it in taking down all of these notes, was an attempt on his part—whether conscious or not—to make sense of, and put together in some kind of a timeline, the events of his life that caused him so much emotional trauma and yet brought him out on the other side with so much love and care from everyone, everywhere.

In my absolutely biased opinion, his truly is a remarkable story. It would be even so if he were not my Grandpa—or my *Grandpeach*, as I used to call him many years ago. That was when I was *Lisach*. Now I'm 56 years old; he's still my Grandpeach, and I'm still his Lisach. After all, we generally remain in a much younger state of mental existence even as our bodies deteriorate and we turn into "old people."

My grandfather is 95 years old now. He just told me over the phone last night that he's basically a shut-in at this point. All of his medical care is brought to him in his Northridge apartment in Jackson Heights (aka East Elmhurst), New York, and he has aides and neighbors coming in to check on him on just about a daily basis. He has Life Alert as well, and my mother Sharon comes to see him weekly. Winter is descending, and he can't leave the house. He's starting to fall a little bit in his apartment now, which is never a good sign. Now is the time to do this and finish it. I'm trying to get this book in his hands by this Christmas.

To My Grandpa

Grandpa, you are very loved. Thank you for telling the story of your life, pushing through all the emotionally painful parts like a soldier, even while people were advising against it so that you would avoid the inevitable anxiety. I know that none of this was easy. You missed two *actual wars* due to different twists of life, and you never got to see the world as a soldier, or what an alternate life might have looked like, but you fought your own wars, and you definitely won.

CHAPTER 1
A Word to the Someones

My name is Arthur Seftel. I want to tell this story, and I feel this story is so unique. I've lived for 94 years, and I've never run into any story like mine, so that's what makes the story unique. There are many "someones" out there, maybe thousands, who have gone through the same thing—and I'm talking about horrible, horrible emotional abuse and neglect—but most probably have not come through it the way I have. Any someones reading this book are going to be all different ages, and I have something to say to the younger ones, and something else to say to the older ones. I hope what I have to say will make a difference for you.

There was a book written not long ago about a young girl, a story set in the Bronx. She was raised by drug addict parents. What she accomplished was living a life a lot like I did, but the only difference between her and me is that I could feel that her parents loved her. There were a lot of similarities in the friends she had. She lived in hallways. Her parents were completely lost to drugs. But what I kept getting from the book, what I got from it was that, especially the mother—they loved their children, but the drugs were too much. It took over their lives. But this young girl did all the things I used to do. She worked any kind of job to make some extra money. When she didn't have a home, she would sleep in different friends' houses. Sometimes she would sleep behind the couch, so the parents of her friends didn't know she was there. The book's name was *Night*. She went on to graduate from Harvard University. She went on to start a foundation to help children like her, kids like her. I was so obsessed with her that I hunted down the name of the organization that she founded, and I called up, wanting to talk to her directly, but a male voice answered instead. I said, "I would like to speak to Miss So-And-So because I was so fascinated by her book." The male who answered said she wasn't available, but he took the time to ask me why I called. It turns out that this man was the woman's closest friend during all of those terrible years, and he ended up becoming the top person in the organization that she founded. I said, are you that "so-and-so" from the book? He laughed and then said, yes, he's the one.

I said to him, "I just want to tell her, as a reader, I have no bad feelings toward her mother. Her mother is fine with me." I'm talking about the drug addict mother. "Because she loved that girl, and it comes through in that story. As a reader, as a victim, I wanted to tell her directly that I love her mother, drug addict and all, despite all the suffering those parents caused." They would steal money from her, all of it. But I didn't have that. I didn't have that love. I had zero—minus zero. All the neglect, but none of the love.

I think a TV movie was made on that story—amazing story. This book affected me deeply, because there were many, many, many similarities. The only other thing she had that I never had was a mentor, and this is really important, even key. If I had had a mentor, even with all other things being equal, I could have gone in a lot of different directions. I had to mentor myself. I view the lack of a mentor as the biggest loss of my life. If the right person had come along, I would have listened to them instead of being such a rebel. If I had had a mentor, I wouldn't have quit school. I never had anyone to guide me, and it was the biggest loss of my life. I couldn't turn to my brothers. They only stayed connected to me when it served their own purposes. I even helped them out with favors and money, even though I was much, much younger than them. But I idolized them; they were my big brothers. But they turned out to be two of the biggest pieces of crap on this planet. Like my therapist said with a sneer, "So much for your heroes." I agreed with her, and I still do.

My hope for someone reading this book, especially if they are a younger person, is that they should understand that I made it, so it *is* possible. But I also want them to know that I feel I only achieved 10% of my potential due to adverse circumstances. On a positive note, I kept out of any trouble and avoided all of the bad kids. So my advice to a young person reading this is: Be careful who your friends are, and stay out of trouble.

I was approached many times by gangs, especially for sports and things like that. They cornered me in the hall, real mob stuff. These were junior high school kids, cornering me to play on their team, but with another agenda attached to it. "I'm with a team," I said, and it was true. But they kept pressuring me. "I just told you, I'm with a team, and I'm not going to leave them." I wasn't caving into the pressure. I'm telling you, they were already with gangs even though this was only junior high. I feel very strongly that the point is to keep out of trouble and work at it—"it" meaning your problems.

You have to do it young. Most kids with my background would get in trouble. It was true then, and it's much truer today. Stay clear and keep away. Most of my friends went to college. There were twelve of us; nine went to college. I felt equal to them. I didn't have the school smarts, but in terms of common sense and intelligence, I was as good as any one of them. They would quiz me when I was 14 and 15 years old and they could never catch me. So to try and stump me, they would give me geometry questions, and I said, "What the hell are you giving me geometry questions for when I can't even spell geometry?" But on the subject of World War II? I *buried* them. I blew them out of the water until it came to geometry. I didn't take any crap from anybody. I was a teenager in an adult world, and I lived like an adult. I thought like an adult, I talked like an adult. I went from 9 to 20 overnight.

If you're an older person, I'd say this: If you haven't tackled all this stuff that I did and you went into adulthood with this abuse like I did, I can only guess that you basically failed. This has to be handled at the beginning of the problem. You can't fix this at 25, 35, 45, and so on, so if you went into your adulthood with this, you're basically a screw-up. I can't tell you there's no hope for you, but I'll tell you this: You would have had to cut it at the root when you were still young yet.

Here's an example. On Wednesday nights, my father and stepmother used to go somewhere. I never had any idea where they went. I didn't have a key because I lost my key, and they never gave me another one because they said I wasn't responsible. So I was locked out of my apartment every Wednesday night. I'm in the hallway of the apartment building every Wednesday night until 2 or 3 o'clock in the morning, and I had to go to school the next day, too. So at 14 years old—and I was working in the pharmacy at the time, too—I get an idea that I'm gonna have dinner on Wednesday nights, because my father and stepmother didn't care when I ate, or even *if* I ate, and they never asked me about it.

Economics was very important then. We were just out of the Depression. I made $3 a week working 36 hours a week. So I went into the bakery and got two kaiser rolls sliced in half. Then I'd go next store to the kosher deli, and I'd get "half a quarter of large bologna." The two rolls were 2 cents each and the "half quarter" was 6 cents, and I figured this out: For a dime (I used to get tips) I'd have dinner. If I had a little extra, I'd get a Pepsi Cola for a nickel.

The heart of the story is this: When the deli owner sliced the bologna, he put the slices one at a time on the scale. When the scale reached "half a quarter" of a pound, he wrapped it up. I'm doing this is for a year. One night, I came in for my dinner and he puts five slices of bologna on the scale. I said, "You have to put another slice." He says, "Can't you read?" So I says, "Every time I get six slices for a half of a quarter and today I get five." He threw the extra slice on the scale, very annoyed. I said, "You know what?

You're not the only deli in Brooklyn. I can take my business elsewhere!" But I got his respect. He didn't push me around.

A passive person is not capable of making waves. They float through their whole life like this. I didn't take crap from anybody. If you don't have the fight in you, nine out of ten of you are going to end up in trouble, wind up in prison, shoot up a school (if it were today), or something like you see in the news every single day. The anger inside of them explodes. It's those parents that cause it. The school doesn't pick it up in time. But the school did try with me; they did notice it, which I'll get into later.

I recommend two things for someone like you— maybe you're one of these passive people who just allowed life to happen to you, and you never asserted yourself or got to the root of the matter: Either go get a mentor, or go get counseling.

There was a very famous person, an author and lecturer named Art Buchwald, whose background was *not* very similar to mine, even though he did have a very tough, tough childhood. He's my age. In his book *Leaving*

Home, he recounts how his mother was put in a mental institution when he was 4 years old, and he had four sisters—horrible, very difficult background. In the 1930s they had the Israel Orphan's Home. That's where you went in the Depression when you couldn't feed your kids. You'd end up in the Orphan's Home and they would foster care you out, or they would keep you and educate you. These kids were caught up during a terrible, terrible time, but they got that help when they were little. The father put the kids in the orphanage only because he had to; he had no choice. But he used to meet them every Saturday in Jamaica, Queens, outside a movie house. The father kept that family alive one day a week for years as they matured. It wasn't a case of parents throwing their kids away. The father just couldn't keep the family together.

But the average 40-year-old today who went through what I went through could not make it if they didn't have some kind of early intervention no matter what their personality was—with no mentor, no early intervention, nothing. I feel like I made it against all odds. I had everything against me. And yet I still don't feel like I actually made it. I will feel forever like I only achieved 10% of my potential. But if could go back and talk to my 14-year-old self and tell him what I know now, my 14-year-old self wouldn't have listened to me anyway. But at least I did see the trouble, and I knew then what I know now—*stay out of trouble*. I was aware that I had to beware, that I had to hang out with the good kids. The kids who played ball.

CHAPTER 2
Earliest Memories

I was born in 1928 and grew up in the Lower East Side of Manhattan. The Lower East Side was Delancey Street to 14th Street North-South, and the East River to the Hudson River in the other direction, so Avenue D to 10th or 11th Avenue. Huge area. The Lower East Side "downtown" area, though, was Delancey Street, Orchard Street, but I lived six or seven blocks away on the numbered streets, where there was a very small Jewish population.

My father was more comfortable with the Polish and Ukrainian population because he came from Poland/Austria (because the borders were constantly changing) and he spoke the language. In that building, there were only about seven Jewish families out of about 50 families. There was a huge church right next to my building. It was very Slavic, the whole block—the funeral parlor, the grocery stores—there were very few Jews in that neighborhood. But it also had a Jewish temple too. There were enough Jews there to have a temple.

One Sunday I was hanging around the church. I was swinging on the open gate, and swinging on the overhead bar. (The gate was usually closed, but it was Sunday.) I was jumping from the steps up to the bar and hanging on it, and that's when these kids surrounded me. They demanded to know, "Are you a Jew?" I knew it had something to do with religion. I thought they were Jews, too, so I made the choice to say "yes," but they threatened me and they said, "If we catch you here again, we're going to beat you up."

I lived in the house next door, 25 feet away. I had no idea what any of this was about. I took a chance that I was making the right choice, but I picked the wrong team.

The enclave I lived in was large. It went from Avenue B all the way to 2nd Avenue—that's *large*. It was at least a square mile of Slavic neighborhood. The kids all spoke English, but every family was bilingual. We spoke Yiddish in my home, and they spoke Polish in theirs. There was a large city park called Tompkins Square Park, which ran from 7th to 10th Street, and from Avenue A to Avenue B, and it's still there. Anything that was happening was happening there: holidays, politicians with their speeches at night—everything happened there.

The Communist Party was big at that time, and there was May Day there every year. Communism was very popular in the 1930s, but it broke up just before World War II. The members were frightened out of it, and they started abandoning it out of fear, but there were still *plenty* of closet Communists after the war. Grandma Rita's parents were into it bigtime.

There was a horse trowel[1] right outside the park, because most of the merchants in those years used horses and wagons. They were lined up halfway down the block. They had the Boys Club of New York on 10th Street. Every kid from about 7 years old and up joined that club, and they had after-school activities there. So there weren't many kids on the street after school. The kids had a really good life, with a lot of activities.

Life was outstanding, actually, for a kid. On summer nights all through the summer, the

---

[1] The term "horse trowel" is intentional. It means "horse trough," but "trowel" is the term that was commonly used at this time, or at least in New York City.

watermelon truck would stop in the middle of the block, and he'd open up the back and slice that watermelon up into all different sizes starting from a penny slice, to a 3-cent slice, and up, and everyone would wait for the watermelon truck.

There were no refrigerators, so you kept stuff cold by buying ice. Every house had a pan to catch the melting water, and in the summer the ice man would come three or four times a day. There was no air conditioning. Only the movie house had it. No other air conditioners.

Flashing forward to when I was in foster care, which I'll talk about some more later in my story, there was a library right across the street from Tompkins Square Park, very close to the family where I was staying as a foster child after my mother died. When I was 10 years old, I walked into that library and opened up a library card for myself, because I needed something to do when I was staying with that family.

The rule was you could take out a maximum of six books each time, and you had to return those books within three weeks. So every three weeks, I took out six books and I read them. By this point, I couldn't read or handle any of what they were giving me in school. But I was an avid reader of these library books, and I gave myself an education. I used to sit in the windowsill and they had a family dog named Tootsie, a bulldog, and this was my reading room, that windowsill. That was my whole life in that foster care situation.

Same sort of thing when I was 7 years old. I walked into the Boys Club of New York when I was 7 years old and told them I was joining. They gave me a nickname—they called me The Midget. This gives you a window into what I was like. I'd walk into places and assert myself, and this is how I survived. It wasn't just how I survived after my mother died when I was 9. I was already trying to survive at an earlier age and insert myself into the fabric of that neighborhood, because the "saintly" ailing mother I had, the one whose altar I had built in my own imagination after she died, believing all that my brothers told me, wasn't such a saint after all. I must have been running from her too.

The household I grew up in was so, so powerful on the negative side. My number one therapist—

her name was Margot, and I saw her for seven years—she never referred to that household as "your home," or "a household," or anything of any kind. She had one reference for that place: "that dark place that you grew up in." She never used the word "family" or anything like that. She said the best thing that ever happened to you is your mother's death. This didn't bother me. You'd think I'd say, "How can you say that to me?" But I was just curious and said, "Why are you saying that?" She said, "If you were brought up in that environment and grew up to full maturity, like those other two"—referring to my brothers—"they are very much alike, aren't they?" she said. And I said, "They *are* alike: both criminal minds."

"You would have been just like them if you grew up in that 'dark place,'" she said. "So much for your heroes."

Because I really idolized them—one eight years older and one twelve years older. They were more parental to me than sibling-like. I thought they were the opposite of those people I despised. Boy was I wrong. She said, "You had to activate your brain in order to survive, once she was gone. Had she lived, and had everything been so-called 'normal,' you would have been like them, and look how they turned out! You brought yourself up: you can't point to someone—anyone—who brought you up, any adult individual who had any connection to your maturity and to bringing you up in the world. And that's how the survival occurred—and that's how *you* occurred—it occurred out of necessity and made you who you are now."

What she said to me came from left field. She just changed the subject midstream and came out with that. She said, "Give me one, just one, instance of a happy moment since the day you were born." And I'm thinking, and I'm quiet. She said, "I'm waiting, and I have the whole session to wait. It's your prerogative. Name just one, a pleasant memory."

I said, "I don't have any."

"How about holiday time?" And she went down the list where you could point to *something*. I said, "Zero." So, she asked me, "Was life so horrible?" And I said, "No. The streets were heaven. All the kids, all the people."

"All the adult people?" "Everyone was wonderful...except that household I came from." Then she went deeper, asking, "What made it so horrible?"

I said to her, "Imagine you are a little boy, and you have two much older brothers, and they're sitting around the dinner table, and conversation is going on all around you, but there is never any conversation going toward you. You become aware of their lives, but you are never, never, ever addressed, not once. What would that do to somebody?"

"I'll tell you one thing it did to you at 4, 5 years old," she remarked. "You'd hold your bowels in on the street." And I did. "Do you have any idea why children do this?" "I don't have a clue," I said. And she said: "That's rage. You were a little kid. You couldn't unleash your rage against these people. This was the only weapon you had." This was a family of five minus one—minus the youngest, who was me.

"What happened if you had an accident?" So I told my therapist that my mother said, "If you do this again, I'm going to wipe your face in it." So she said, "That's not exactly a way to reduce rage or even address rage. It's just rage turned into more rage and more rage."

Then she dug even further. "What was your relationship with your friends on the street?" "Mostly it was okay," I said, "but there were flashes of anger in the game-playing." "You grew up with rage," she said. "Your formative years were all rage."

My mother already had breast cancer before I was even born. She got pregnant at 38 and died nine years later. So she was pregnant with cancer, and she had two sons long before I was born: my brother Sid, who was 8 when I was born, and my half-brother Harry, who was 12 when I was born. So by the time I was 5, I had teenage brothers and two parents in their 40s. My brothers fit in with my parents, and were more parental than brotherly—they didn't fit in with me at all and were totally disinterested in me. I had to have been an accident, because I was a nonentity. I didn't fit into that household. *At all.*

They were all adults, and I was this little kid. This created an anger, an anger that I discussed in therapy. I had nothing in common with this adult family. They were totally disinterested in this 4-, 5-year old-child, but they all had common interests, and they were a family unit in every way. The child was not involved in *any* way. I was an orphan sitting at the table with them.

My earliest memory was lying in a brown crib in a yellow room. I remember my room clearly. It was yellow, and it was separated by glass panes that looked into a dining room. There was no such thing as a living room like we have now. It was called a dining room and it had a big dining room table. From the dining room it went into the kitchen. The kitchen was nothing remarkable. It had a table, a chair, and not a refrigerator—it was an ice box. You bought ice from the ice man. He would sell you a piece of ice: a penny, a nickel, a dime. Depending on what you paid, you would get that size of ice. You could even get fruit by the slice: a penny or a nickel. Same thing with cigarettes: you could by one cigarette if you wanted, and they were called "loosies." A penny for one or 20 cents for a pack. That was during the Depression.

These were European parents who came to this country. They were much, much more European than American. They were from Poland/Austria, that area. They were 5% American and 95% where they came from. I remember they were very, very short—5 foot, 2 inches short. When they spoke English it was broken English. They were completely fluent when it was Yiddish or Polish. They spoke to their children in broken English, and they were answered in English.

My parents were a unit within a unit; they spoke to each other in a language that none of the children spoke or understood. They would get mail from Europe—their families all remained in Europe, and they were all killed in the Holocaust. That rendered us children zero relatives. No aunts, no uncles, no cousins, nobody by the time the war ended. I didn't understand any of the

Polish, but as a 5-year-old, I did pick up some of the Yiddish—not totally. I couldn't pick it up enough to speak it, but I could understand about 50% of it.

The Polish was out of the question. They spoke it when they had something private to say to each other and they didn't want any of us to understand. It was not a warm place, not an affectionate place. My father owned a window-cleaning business serving small businesses, and he had a window cleaning route. My mother was a housewife with cancer. I was born to a mother with breast cancer, and I assume she became pregnant with the breast cancer as an older mother—she was about 38 or 39 when I was born. I remember staring at that removed breast when I was little, when she would take off her shirt and walk around like that. More on that later.

Dinner was always a long affair—a lot of talking, talking, talking. There was zero subject matter where I could ever be involved. The ignoring of me was so deep and profound that it was unreal. Nobody asked me about school. They asked their two sons, the adults, how was your day? I would just sit there.

To go into it more deeply, as to what was it like sitting at the table for an hour and a half, and you are completely out of everything the entire time, every day ... what did I do during that time? I listened to and got lost in *The Make Believe Ballroom* radio show hosted by Martin Block. I would concentrate on the music the whole time I was sitting at the table. I had nothing to do with the conversation or the people at that table, and to this day, the music has that same meaning to me.

When I sit around in my apartment now, and it's quiet, I have that music on. I learned all the lyrics, the music of the day. The same as they shut me out, I shut them out. I used to wait for the music to come on. So whatever transpired at that table, after a while it didn't bother me anymore, because I became lost in the music and I shut them out. I wasn't directly hurt at the table by the neglect, or I was too young to feel it at the time ... because I was just too young. The music was my substitute. They shut me out, and I shut out the talking. Everything was music for that hour and a half. It made it pleasant for me; I waited for it every night.

My father got up at 5 o'clock in the morning, every morning, and would wrap his arm in the *tefillin*, and he would chant, and he was deeply religious, but at the same time, I was a victim of his rottenness and his meanness, and I thought, "How can you be such a religious and God-fearing person and be so rotten in other aspects of your life?" I had a terrible, terrible life because of him, and at the same time he had these deep religious beliefs—very devout—and my mother did the candles every Friday at sundown. They followed everything to the letter as far as a religion. But how could he be a monster to his children, break up the house the way he did, and act like everything was okay?

My therapist, who I saw for years and years, diagnosed him as having severe narcissistic personality disorder. It was really severe. It shook up the counselor herself. She would shake her head at some of the things he did, especially after my mother died. And he did the *same things* after his first wife died, when my oldest brother was left as a 2-year-old. He did the same thing that he did to me: He handed my brother over to his late wife's family. By brother later joined the family when he was 7.

I called my brother up when he was in his 80s and I asked him, "How come you weren't in the pictures?" He said, "For five years I was with my mother's family. Every six months they put me in a new family in a new house, with a new neighborhood. For five years."

My therapist went berserk when she heard this story, that this could happen to a child in his formative years. And my brother ended up being a nut when he was an adult—serious problems. As soon as the mother is gone, you start a new family, and you start from scratch. You dump your kid, and you start a new family. The same thing he did to my brother, he did to me. Only he was 2 and I was 9. My brother was bounced around every six months for five years. I only stayed with my foster family for six months, and then they told my father that he had to come get me. They wanted me out of there.

CHAPTER 3
My Mother and My Old Neighborhood

If your room had a window that faced the street I was called the "front room". Modern apartments are different, but back then they were called railroad flats. You went from room to room to room. You came into a kitchen from the hall but you had to go from room to room like a railroad car. All of these railroad flats were the same.

It was very common for people to look for boarders. They looked for single people who would live with families for economic reasons. We didn't need a boarder because my father had a window cleaning business. He had a route cleaning windows for small mom-and-pop stores around the neighborhood. But my father loved money, so he got one anyway. Our boarder had a key to a bedroom that was in our apartment. It was a strange setup. You could get to his bedroom through our apartment or through the hallway, so we never saw him. He was a waiter in the neighborhood restaurant.

[*What are the main things you remember from that time period?*]

The main things I remember from that time period, up to the age of 5, were three things.

One

When my mother went shopping every day, she left me alone. This was preschool. She would come home with a big shopping bag. I was angry that she had to go shopping. I could hear the kids out on the street playing, and I used to go to the window. I used to yell at them, "Don't start any games until I come down!!" They started hide-and-seek and jump rope, and it *killed* me, because she wasn't back yet.

Here's another game they used to play: Potsie. You would take the skin of an orange—not the whole orange, just a piece. All the kids carried chalk with them; almost every game required chalk. So on the sidewalk, you would draw a white line down the center of a piece of sidewalk. The closer half you put a number 1 and the half farther away you put a number 2, and then you keep going: 3 and 4, and then you'd make a 5 and 6. Everyone tossed the orange peel into the 1 and then would hop into the 1, bend down and pick up the orange peel, and keep hopping.

There was a rest stop at number 3. You didn't have to stay on one leg at the rest stop. There was also a rest stop at number 6. Then you had to hop back again. This was a big, big game for the kids.

At night, another very popular game was called Actors and Actresses. So "JD" would be Jimmie Durante. It was a sitting-around game. You had to guess the identity of the actor or actress. CG was Clark Gable. Whoever guessed correctly was the next person to choose the initials. We played this game a lot.

But the *really* big game was hide and seek. But because of the Depression era, a lot of families who didn't pay their rent for three months were evicted. So there were families out on the street with all their furniture. So this was great for the kids, because we had all kinds of places to hide: Behind the couch, behind the dresser. It could be a family of seven or eight and they were all out on the street. One day they were there with all their furniture, and then someone would come by and they were gone, along with all their furniture. It had to be some kind of an agency like the Red

Cross. They weren't out there for more than 24 hours.

I remember my mother in those first five years ... maybe when I was 2. I remember *seeing her*. When the three men were gone, I remember her parading around the house in her panties only, and just on the bottom. On the top she wasn't wearing anything. And she had her one breast removed. She had this ugly, ugly wound, something horrible to look at. I knew that what I was looking at was something horrible and ugly, but I didn't know *what* I was looking at. It was just ... an ugly, ugly, ugly thing. I remember that clearly. It was like she came back from the store, and she would change and walk around in her panties. Maybe she was a nut job. I don't know.

Two

The next thing I can recall is the cancer treatments, and my memories of being taken to the facility where she was treated. The memory of being alone for what seemed like an eternity in a room all by myself with chairs, about a dozen chairs, and there was nobody there, no medical people, nobody, and that was the room I sat to wait for her, with nothing to do, while she went for her treatments. It was uncomfortable—not dramatic, not terrible—but I *hated* going there because I had nothing to do, and I had no way of judging time back then. I don't remember if we went once a week or twice a week, but I do know I hadn't started school yet. We didn't take the bus, because we didn't want to spend the money. She walked 19 blocks there and 19 blocks back. I'm thinking now: We weren't destitute—she was able to fill up her shopping bags with plenty of food—and I could have ridden for free. The whole thing would have cost 10 cents round trip. I don't know why she never took the bus. We also had an El train. Maybe my father told her to walk. It's very possible. He loved money.

Three

I remember dinner at the kitchen table, seven nights a week. I don't know how long the dinners lasted, but my memory tells me the dinners lasted a long time. All they talked about was themselves and their lives. Everything was the four lives, every night, at the dinner table, but nothing involving me: zero. My older brother

Harry, when he came home for dinner, he would put on the radio, and on the radio would be Martin Block's *Ballroom*. This radio program was very, very big at the time. All the teenagers who were into music and dancing had that station on. Benny Goodman, Glenn Miller, Tommy Dorsey, Jimmy Dorsey, Chick Webb.

When the radio came on, I shut them all out. It explains my love of music to this day. That's where I got that from. I shut them out the way they shut me out. Every night this lasted for an hour and a half to two hours—talk, talk, talk—but was I asked about school? *Never.* I was a nonentity, a piece of furniture.

CHAPTER 4
No Saint to Look Back on

When my therapist asked me if I had ever had even just *one* pleasant memory growing up, I couldn't think of a single one, and this is why: There were no holidays, no birthdays. Just anger.

I can prove it, and the therapist agreed with me. This was all when I was 5 years old and under. I will prove it to you. I'd hold my bowels in, and then I'd have accidents in my pants. I learned much later on that I was doing this out of anger; the therapist told me it was actually called "rage." My mother threatened me one time that she was going to wipe it in my face, and that one time came: She held the underwear in her hand and rubbed the contents all over my face.

Another time, my mother and I were going to a grocery store that was pretty far from the house. I don't know why she went that distance. It was about five blocks away, but these were long blocks. It was the only time she ever went there, and she had to pass so many other stores to get there. So there was a display for animal crackers. I reached for the box and she said, "You can't have any." I reached for it again, and she said no. So I had a tantrum in the street and wouldn't walk. I threw myself in the street, and she dragged me home the entire five blocks. I remember being dragged by one arm, screaming the whole time. When we got to our building, I finally stood up. I stood up, and then I ripped my shirt; I popped all the buttons off my shirt out of sheer rage. I don't remember ever getting a beating, though. I don't remember anything happening to me after this happened. I don't remember ever getting spanked, which was unusual for that time period.

The lack of any kind of verbal interaction with my mother, or any sense of her involvement with me in a normal mother-son relationship became so clear when neighbors would come by the apartment. At about the same time as the shirt-ripping incident, when I was around 4 or 5 years old, I remember his older lady named Minnie. She used to fuss over me; she would pinch my cheeks and scream up to God about how cute I was, but I clearly remember my mother hanging back, with her back up against the wall during those sessions. She looked so uncomfortable.

She never joined in with them to fuss over me, not even to keep up appearances. She always seemed so uncomfortable and always had a strange look on her face when they did that.

Cigarette Packets and a Lost Silver Ball

Everyone smoked in those days. And everyone, when they finished a pack, would throw it in the gutter. I started collecting the thrown-away packs of cigarettes. Nobody ever asked me where I was. I would walk from 7th to 14th street, and at 14th Street I would cross 1st Avenue, 2nd Avenue, 3rd Avenue... 14th Street was a major street, it was like Times Square in that neighborhood—the lower East side, where I grew up. So I remember that when I was about 5 years old, and before I had started kindergarten, I would walk everywhere and stuff my pants pockets with these cigarette packs. Then I would go back into the apartment, and into the bathroom, and I would empty my pockets. I would then fill up the sink with hot water. The hot water allowed me to peel the silver paper away from the wax paper on the cigarette packs to make a silver ball. All the other parts of the packs I managed to throw in the bathroom garbage can without my mother seeing anything. I don't remember what the goal was, but the silver ball became pretty big. I don't know what happened to it.

I remember those walks to get the cigarette packs, at least 10 blocks—again, this was before I even started kindergarten. I took these walks in the morning, early in the day. But my mother had no idea I was doing stuff like this, and she never knew where I was or asked. I don't know anyone else who had a silver ball, or how I got this into my head to do this. Whenever I walked back, I took the opposite side of the street so I could maximize the number of cigarette packs that I'd be able to bring back. I'd crush the packs and squeeze them.

How I Accidentally Became a Shabbos Goy

On Fridays at sundown, my mother would light the candles for Shabbos and say the prayers, waving her arms ... all that stuff. She baked the challah in those days, but after a while, as she was getting sicker, I used to go and buy it for her. She would give me 15 cents to buy the challah for Shabbos. I grew up in a very kosher house.

When I was young, I remember one of the neighbors calling me into her house on Fridays. She would give me a penny to turn the lights on or off—my first job—she must have thought I was a Shabbos goy, or she didn't care, but she gave me that penny and I would take it and buy a chocolate bar. It was a knockoff of the Nestle bar; it was called Hooten. If I had had 2 cents put together, I would have bought the Nestle bar. The Hooten bar was nowhere near as good.

Growing Up on the Lower East Side

We lived on the third floor. The ice cream man used to come around in a cart on the back of a bicycle, and he would ring his bell. I would yell up to my window, "Throw me down a penny," and my mother would wrap the penny up in brown paper and throw it out the window, so that it would float and not go all over the place. And I remember getting that penny to get an ice cream from that cart.

A little more background about the neighborhood I lived in while my mother was still alive: In those days, there were still horses and buggies all over the place. I remember the horse trowels on the street where the horses would drink. The wagons would be lined up, and I used to love to watch the horses line up and drink. We had a lot of horses and wagons back then for almost anything: food, clothing, anything—sharpening scissors, sharpening knives.

The watermelons were on trucks. They would come at night when everyone was out on hot summer nights. Even though there were trucks, there were far more horses and wagons, because gas was so expensive. In the summertime, the ice men were busy from morning to night, and everyone had pans under their ice boxes to catch the melting water. The ice man didn't have any delivery method other than carrying a big ice chunk up to each apartment. They would put it on their shoulder wrapped in a thick blanket, and they would carry it on their backs to their customers.

Everyone was on the roofs of the building on hot days, and it was like the beach up there. Nobody locked their doors either. Everyone would meet their neighbors on the roof with their bottles of water because nobody had air conditioning yet. The only places that had air conditioners at that time were the movie houses. Nobody had it in their house. So people would go to the movies like crazy—if for nothing else, just to cool off. Movies were about a dime at the time.

The Day I Almost Died

When I was about 8 years old, maybe younger, we were in Coney Island for the summer, renting a room from a private family who lived there. People did anything to make a buck during the Depression. My mother and I would be there all week long, and my brothers and father would come once a week, every Saturday and Sunday. I would go to the beach by myself, and the beach was four to five blocks away, with all of Coney Island only being about seven blocks total. I'd put on my bathing suit and would cross major thoroughfares, similar to Queens Boulevard or Times Square today.

I would be gone all morning, and I would go out only in my bathing suit, no top. My mother never asked me where I was, where I was going, or what I was doing. I never remember a single conversation with her that summer. She knew I was going to the ocean alone, and she didn't ask questions or care that I was doing this.

I used to play this game of walking backwards into the ocean, two or three steps at a time, and then I'd take another step back and it would be up to my face, and I would keep taking steps back and make sure I could feel the ground each time.

But this one time that summer I couldn't feel the ground anymore, and I was in over my head. The thing that saved me was that I used to watch how the swimmers swam, I used to watch them carefully. So when I didn't feel the ground anymore, I started using my arms like the swimmers do, I did the same thing and I felt I was slowly moving back to shore. I could feel my arms moving in a swimming motion; the scary part was that I couldn't get my body flat to kick my legs in a lying-down position. I didn't panic because I could see I was creeping little by little with my arms. And then suddenly I felt the ground. And I remember that at that moment, the first thing I said to myself was, "I will never do anything like this this again." I finished the summer vacation there, but I never did this again.

But it still stays with me that nobody ever asked me where I was going or what I was doing that summer, not even when my father and brothers would come there on the weekends.

The Time I Took My Problems Out on a Kitten

There was one very bizarre incident that happened that summer. On my way to the beach one day, I passed an apartment that looked abandoned. I heard a cat crying through the window, and I climbed in and took the kitten and climbed out. And I walked to the bay, seven blocks opposite the ocean, and I threw the cat into the bay. It had to be that *rage*. That's exactly what it was. I hid when I saw the commotion. I wanted to see what the outcome was going to be. I didn't want to be caught or seen, but I could see everything that was happening. I could see the people running, and they did save the kitten. I don't even know why I did it. I wasn't planning to kill the kitten, but I just impulsively did it. It wasn't like me to do this. If I were just a completely noncaring person, I wouldn't have stuck around to see what would happen. And I think I remember I felt a little bit of relief that they saved it.

The Neighborhood Girls Who Sat With Me

Times were so bad leading up to my mother's decline, that if weren't for these two girls in the neighborhood, who were two to three years older than me, I'm not sure what I would have done.

Their names were Pauline and Ette. They used to sit outside with me on the stoop until 8, 9 o'clock at night, and they'd *talk* to me. Everyone in the neighborhood by this point knew my mother was dying, but these two girls really took the time to talk to me, and stay with me—to give me some level of affection and attention that I never was able to get at home, and it brought me through a very dark time. I don't know why their names are just popping into my mind now, about 85 years after the fact. It's amazing the effect and impact some people can have on other people's lives while they are completely unaware of the healing that came through them, even if only temporary.

CHAPTER 5
My Mother's Death

My mother wound up, just before she died, in place called Welfare Island. Welfare Island is an island under the 59th Street Bridge, which connects Manhattan to Queens. The island, uninhabited at the time except for the hospital is now called Roosevelt Island. They developed it about 20 to 30 years later, and a lot of people live there now. But during the Depression, people who were dying without having the money to go to a decent hospital ended up there. So my mother ended up in a place for destitute people, even though my father probably did have the money to send her somewhere else, since my family was relatively unaffected by the Depression. He must not have wanted to spend the money on her.

In her final days, we used to go there once or twice a week. She didn't last long there, maybe a couple of months. We all used to take a trolley car from 59th Street and 2nd Avenue—they had a trolley running across that bridge into Queens. The trolley would stop right in the center of the bridge, and we would then get off the trolley and onto an elevator that would take us down to the Island. It was a massive elevator, big enough to hold about 100 people. And we would get off the elevator and walk about half a mile to the hospital. We would get there, and there would be about 1,000 people, all dying, as far as the eye could see—all of them were dying. It was an unreal sight to see that. They were all on cots, no beds. And every visit, the three of them would be around the bed, and it was the same foursome, the same family, that same close-knit family that used to talk around the dinner table for hours. They didn't even realize I wasn't there when I would hang back. That part was okay with me, because I didn't want to be around there at all, and I couldn't wait to get out of there.

The last time we went, in April 1938, she was very, very, very weak. I could see this clearly from a distance, and she died shortly after that visit. Suddenly, this last time, she knew I was there. She very weakly started pushing them aside; she wanted to see me, but she couldn't see me because they were all around her bed. So she pushed one aside to the right—I think it was my brother Sid—and then she pushed another one aside to the left. I was about 10 to

15 feet away from the bed, and she motioned to me to come over to her. That was the first time ever, in all the visits, that she had wanted to see me. I knew this was the last time I was ever going to see her, so I approached the bed.

The self-consciousness I experienced was horrible. I wanted to sink through a hole in the floor. I walked up to the bed, and she put her fingers to my face and felt all around my face with her fingers. It made me so uncomfortable; it was like a stranger touching my face. She couldn't talk anymore, so that was the only contact or form of communication. And then that was the end. She died on April 27, 1938.

There was a funeral, and it was terrible. It was a religious funeral, a nightmare. And they sat shiva for seven days. The whole thing was a nightmare. It was a horror for me. By September or October of the same year, my father already had a girlfriend and was breaking up the family. I went into foster care in October 1938. I was 10 years old.

CHAPTER 6
School Life in the Early Years, and Getting Lost in the Silver Screen

Looking back, school was good in my early years. I remember kindergarten, but not my first day of kindergarten. I have this isolated memory that there was a black kid in my kindergarten class, and I had never seen a black kid before in my life. This tells you something about the time period. They partnered us up for the whole term, and the rule was that we were to hold hands everywhere we went. And every time he let go of my hand, I used to smell my hand, and I remember my hand smelled like my mother's chicken soup. Just a random memory.

I was in the "1" class, the so-called "smart class." From first grade on, I remember going home for lunch by myself, and I don't remember anyone taking me to or from school, which was four blocks away from home. All the kids were safe; everyone was safe. The point of telling this part of my story—how I had a really good relationship with and attitude toward school—will become a lot more apparent later in my story.

These years were heaven and hell at the same time. They were hell at home, but as soon as I walked out the door I had total freedom, and the whole world was wide open to me. Kids these days went to the movies alone, not with a parent, and I was going to the movies all by myself from the time I was 7 or 8 years old. We all used to get lost in the movies the way I'd get lost in *The Make Believe Ballroom*. It was one of the big, big highlights.

I remember we used to stand around the box office and yell, "Take me in, take me in!" A matron would come out and take the kids away from the adults and put them in the children's section of the movies. So little children were able to go to the movies completely safely. I was in the movies *constantly*—we all were. It couldn't have been more than 10 cents to get in. The kids would go in the daytime, and you'd be there for four hours. They would show something called "chapters" (like Flash Gordon, Tailspin Tommy, Dick Tracey), double features, cartoons, news reels, all kinds of stuff on the screen, and the parents would be able to get rid of their kids for at least four to five hours. There was always a cliff hanger for the chapters and sometimes you would have to go back 20 or 30 times to see the end of the chapters. Nobody would miss a chapter.

I remember going to a movie with a neighbor of mine one time. My name was "Bummie" (nickname for Arthur) and his name was "Shmeelik" (nickname for Sidney). We never used our American names when we were among ourselves. (Incidentally, my legal name ended up as Arthur because my brothers talked my parents out of naming me Abraham.) So we were carrying on one day, and the matron told us she was going to throw us out—and she did. So we're walking home and we are both laughing our heads off, because we saw the chapter and she didn't know that when she threw us out! That part was the best part, and she thought she was punishing us! I'll never get over that memory: We put something over on that matron, and we laughed the whole way home.

The theater was called The Hollywood. And outside on Avenue A, it was all trolley cars. There were no buses yet in those days. The trolley cars were colorful—green and yellow on the outside—and they made a lot of noise. I never rode those trolleys. I walked everywhere.

There was one trolley car that ran across the East River. To ride it, you had to pay 3 cents; if you kept going into Brooklyn, you had to pay another 2 cents. You used to have to put the money right into the trolley driver's hand when you boarded the trolley, because there was no receptacle into which the money could be deposited. But I used to walk over the Williamsburg Bridge into Brooklyn. It was two or three miles, and that was nothing for a kid. I just crossed the bridge for the sake of it. I liked the walk. It was a big wide walkway. I had nothing I needed to do in Brooklyn. Everything in those years ... you were safe. *Everything*.

Parenting Was Different Back Then

There was a bad kid on the block. The police picked him up and they took him to the police station, which was on 5th Street between 1st and 2nd Avenue. He was about 9 years old, and he was gone for about two hours. Suddenly he was coming back and he was all disheveled and he was crying. He was walking back by himself. I see his mother standing there, watching. Her arms are folded and she is expressionless. He's wiping his eyes and his shirt is hanging out. They must have beaten him up. There was a small crowd of kids, and we were all watching to see what his mother was going to do. She gave him such a slap in his face, because she was mortified that this happened. She didn't go to a lawyer for a lawsuit against the police. She took it out on him. And from that day on he was a different kid. He never got in any more trouble after that. She really gave him a shot. That would have been a juicy lawsuit today.

CHAPTER 7
The Day My Father Broke Up the Family

About a year ago I was having frequent anxiety problems, and they were triggered by the stress of taking care of Grandma. My doctor put me on Ativan, three pills a day, maximum, as needed, but fortunately I was able to get away with one pill, the smallest dose. Anyone who needs three pills, I feel sorry for those people—especially when they take it in the daytime. It knocks you out. It's a great sleeping pill.

So here's the story: I know my doctor for about 30 years, and he says, "Look, I don't talk about your background. I know your outline. I have no reason to go into what happened to you as a child. I don't have to add anything to what I know about you. But recently, up until recently, you don't need the Ativan. Do you think this is mainly because of Grandma's condition?" I said, "I think it's not mainly that but partly that."

But I belong to this organization NORC,[2] and they have these graduate students who are going for their master's degrees. In their fifth

---
[2] Naturally Occurring Retirement Communities.

year they come to NORC so they can work with live people. They are very good, and they are graduate students coming from NYU and Columbia (the one from Columbia was my all-time favorite), and I said to him, "What I'm slowly finding when I'm working with these young ladies for a couple of years now—the anxiety has increased, and it's *gotta* be something else beyond just taking care of Grandma."

He said, "Look, you went through trauma as a child. What that was doesn't matter for this conversation. You have to be aware that when you dredge up the past, if something happens—you're over 90 years old, and you're talking about something that happened 80 years ago—you would think that this happened way back and everything else, but your subconscious has a life of its own. There's a conscious, and we have a *subconscious*. You could be talking to these people, these young ladies, and they're asking these probing questions, and you could be stirring up, unbeknownst to you, a hornet's nest, and it's buried where you buried them, but it's also with you all the time."

He asked me what I generally talk about with my friends, and I said, "They talk about the past, because they don't have a future and they don't have a present." So he said, "The less you dig up the past, the lower your anxiety, but you're increasing your anxiety, and this is a warning: this is the way the subconscious works; if it's something severe and it's laying quiet for the last 65 years, and suddenly you're getting these bouts of anxiety, that's where it's coming from. I'd advise you not to go back into your childhood if you can help it." And I'd have to agree with him. Dormant is not dead.

Saying this out loud I have to pinch myself. But there was one point in my 20s or so—and I said this to Grandma once—I said, "If I had to do everything over again, one thing I think I would do differently," and this shocked her, "I would have stayed with my father and stepmother, because the worst thing I ever did was move in with my brother." She was in total shock, but I said, "I'm really serious."

When my mother was really sick and getting sicker, and when she was dying, it was a crisis. When she died—she died on April 27—April,

May, June, July, maybe August, we were surviving the death. For instance at this point I was now 10, my brothers were adults, and my father was working in his window-cleaning business. We were making it, actually. It was 1938, and the Great Depression was in its last two to three years or so, because Pearl Harbor was around the corner, and that ended the Depression. But in my household, the Depression didn't really affect us because my father had his own business. My older brother was 21 and had his own job.

The Conversation and the Break

But what happened was, I was in class 6B, 10 years old, and this would have been in September or October when this happened. One night—I was in bed, because I had to go to school the next day, and my two brothers were in the living room with my father—I start hearing a conversation. My father said to my two brothers: "You have to get out of the house, because I'm breaking up the apartment, and you have to find someplace to live."

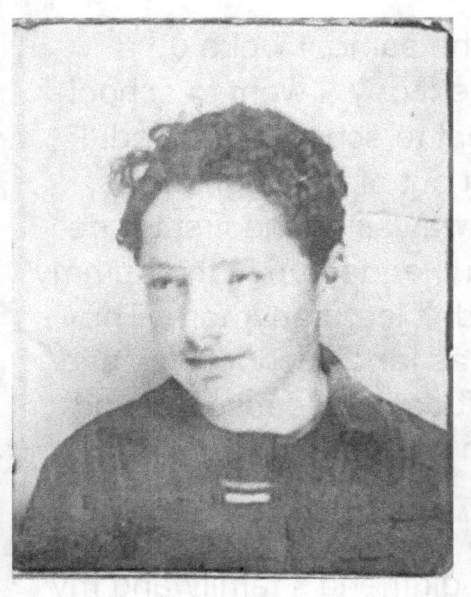 I went into something beyond shock at what I was hearing. I can't even find the word that I'm looking for: it was surreal what I was hearing. And I had the worst attack imaginable, much stronger than a panic attack. Not even "terror" could describe it. I became hysterical in my bed. It was 8 o'clock at night. I started to say over and over again, "I don't want to go, I don't want to go, I don't want to go..." to the point where even if someone would have tried to, nothing could have snapped me out of the state I was in. I think it was a Wednesday night.

Suddenly a door opened and the full light of the living room came into the bedroom. I don't know who was standing in that doorway, which one of the three of them. And they said, "That's enough already. Shut up and go to sleep." And I shut up instantly. And everything stopped from that point on. And I was never the same. I woke up a different person the next day. I went to school the next day, but I went to school damaged. I ended up being taken out of the bright class, which I was in all the way since the first grade. But I couldn't function. I ended up in the dummy class, because I couldn't learn anymore. The only motivation I had as far as school was after that was not to get left back, because nothing else would have been worse than that.

For six months, when I was 10, my father put me in foster care with his girlfriend's family and my brothers were kicked out of the house. If you can picture this, physically the whole family was within two blocks of each other after the split-up, but there was no contact. I never saw my brothers after that. I had no idea what any of them were doing, including my father. He took a furnished room for himself until he could marry his girlfriend.

The foster care people put him up against a wall. They said, "When are you talking your kid out of here?" He was prepared to leave me there for good. He was paying them, and he figured they would want to make a buck so they could just keep me. He must have told them that when he gets married, he will take me back, but he never did. So they forced him to take me out of there. Because they had five kids of their own and they had money problems.

But my stepmother resented me from day one. She said to him, "I'll marry you if there are no kids." So when he took me back in, she took her anger out on me. They both did. And yet, I told Grandma, if I had to do this over again, I never would have gone to my brother to get away from them.

CHAPTER 8
Life in Foster Care

I went into foster care in December 1938, eight months after my mother died. I was there for six months, from December through May 1939. The father in this house had five kids, his mother-in-law (old gray-haired lady), and his wife, and I'm in this place, and the rooms are the size of closets. The father was *not* in favor of this arrangement.

He was a big, big hulking man, about 6 foot, 2 inches and maybe 230 pounds—a big, big man. I was only 10 years old. In my eyes, he was a giant. It was a memorable experience. I had to sleep with him because of his religious beliefs. This was an Ultra-Orthodox household. The husband and wife don't sleep together apparently—not during the week, anyway. The first night I'm there, I'm against the wall, and he's next to me, and I have to go to the bathroom. I had no idea how to get out of the bed, because I'm afraid of waking up the "Monster." I'm in a strange house, and I'm in a predicament. I finally figured out that if I go to the front of the bed instead of the side, I'd just have to climb over the metal front of the bed. And I managed to do it, and climb back.

This was a cold water flat, and the bathroom is in the hall. The bathroom is the only bathroom on that floor, and there were about six to eight apartments on that floor. Everyone had to use it—and I keep calling it a "bathroom," but it wasn't. It was a toilet and a flush, not even a sink. Everybody on that floor had only *that* to use on that floor—a cold water flat in the middle of the Depression.

So that first night when I went into that bathroom, I was barefoot, and it was freezing. This became a ritual, every night going to the bathroom once or twice without waking up the monster. He was a scary-looking guy.

It was obvious that this foster care arrangement was the mother's idea. The mother was related to my father's new girlfriend (and later wife) in some way. They were likely cousins, and the arrangement prevailed even though the husband was against it. My father came around to pay them once a month for six straight months and never once asked for me or about me, never asked if I was comfortable, nothing. But it didn't bother me because I was used to him. I knew what he was.

This family would talk about my situation in Yiddish, and they would say, "When is he gonna take his kid out of here?" They had no idea I understood enough Yiddish to understand what they were saying. They would talk about me being there so long while sitting at the kitchen table, after I would go to bed. But I understood every word.

My father had promised this family that he would come get me after he got married and settled. But he got married and he never came back for me, like he promised. After six months, on the day he went to pay them, they finally confronted him: "When are you going to take your kid?" This was the Depression, and they had their own problems—five kids in a cold water flat, and all the rest. They wanted me out of there; they had no room for me. But they had to put my father up against a wall and *force* him to take me. If he had had his way, he would have left me there. That was his game plan.

There were seven or eight people living in a closet in this place. It was awful. My "room" was a wide windowsill. But at least I was close enough to my old neighborhood to see my friends and everything else—that was the only normal part of this whole experience.

There was another silver lining to that foster care situation. While I was in foster care, I asked them if I could have a library card, and they said yes. So I walked into the library and got myself a library card, and I asked the librarian how many books I could take out at time, and for how long. They said I could take out six books at time and could keep them for six weeks.

I never partook of their family discussions—I was completely alone there too, and I didn't want to bother with them anyway. They were really devout. They wore yarmulkes, and some of them wore hats in the house. And they were in there davening—a lot of davening going on in that house. But I kept to myself, because I wasn't interested in any of that stuff.

The windowsill was this wide windowsill, and I'm little; I'm 10 years old. I was able to keep the books there, and there was still room for me, with the books, to sit on the windowsill with my knees bent to prop up the book, and that's what I'd do every spare minute in that house. I'd take no part in anything there. But I remember though, very fondly, that they had a dog, a bulldog, and they needed a dog like they needed a hole in the head. The bulldog's name was Tootsie. When I was sitting and reading, that dog would be by my side. Even three hours later, that dog would still be by my side. I'd turn the page with my right hand and reach down and pet her head with my left hand. She never left my side.

CHAPTER 9
The Nightmare Years

After my father took me out of foster care, the next six years were a nightmare until I finally moved out on my sixteenth birthday. The time spent in that even *darker* place in Brooklyn, the new apartment in Bensonhurst that he was living in with his new wife, was without a doubt the worst experience of my life. Moving to Brooklyn was like moving to a foreign country at first, but my fondest memories—outside of the house— did end up coming from that place. It was heaven out on the streets.

Making Deals With God

There was nobody else to talk to in the new apartment. At night, I'd have these conversations with God. It was always the same theme:

> "I'm not going to get into trouble or do anything wrong or bad. I'm asking, God, if you could take care of me. I promise I won't do anything wrong or bad, and that I will be a good kid."

And God would take care of me. This deal-making with God was my way of coping with the situation. It was a real relationship I had with God, seven nights a week. To me, I felt God would take care of me, and I tried to be as good as I could be in terms of choosing friends. I was very conscious of trying to be the best I could be, and that God was taking care of me. I made God my mentor because I never had one—*and I just realized that*. Through God, I was holding myself to a much higher standard. God was my mentor, because I made it through, through that storm. He kept me on the straight and narrow.

The Day I Tried to Run Away from Home

I was in that apartment for only a few months when I had had enough, and it came into my head to run away. I was only 10 years old. One day at about 4 o'clock in the afternoon, I was outside in the neighborhood, and the weather was warm—I remember that clearly—and I get this idea that I'm going to walk to my brother Sidney's house. That was my game plan. I had no money. All I needed was a nickel for the car fare, but I didn't have it. I could have succeeded; I could have just taken the subway, because I knew the entire New York subway system completely, and I knew how to get to my brother's house by train because I took the train to his house every week. But I didn't have a nickel, and I didn't want to go back to the house either. I wanted so badly not to go back there to ask for money that I decided to walk. From Brooklyn to Manhattan.

I figured out the direction into Manhattan because I knew the direction of the train lines. So I found myself walking and walking … and it's getting dark. I would say that after three hours of walking, I knew this is not going to work. I didn't know where I was. I wasn't lost, because I knew I was still in Brooklyn, but I knew that this can't work, so I had no choice but to go home.

When I got home, she blew her stack. I don't remember what she said, but it wasn't pleasant, that's for sure. There was no fear in her face or in her voice—just anger. I did not answer her. I was just silent. I didn't say a word to her. The whole thing was my attempt to escape, and it didn't work. And from that point on, when I went to my brother's house by train, it didn't occur to me to refuse to go home.

The Roses Who Tried to Help Me

The first Rose, I'll call her Mallomar Rose, was possibly my mother's cousin, but I can't be sure exactly how she was related to me. But I know that she went back many, many years with my family. When my mother was alive, we used to visit her house in Brooklyn very regularly.

I went to see this Rose every week, every Tuesday and every Thursday, from age 10 to age 12, and she would feed me Mallomars, which were my favorite, and she would vent to me about my father. These visits were my idea. I hunted her down right after I moved into that apartment in Bensonhurst, and I initiated these get-togethers to escape from the apartment. I told her, "I live close to you, and could we do this." I went on to tell her what was going on in that house, and how I felt, and how terrible it was, and she gladly agreed to the twice-weekly visits.

Rose had a hatred for my father that was so deep that she would spend half the time I was there venting about how horrible he was. I think if she had had a knife in her hand and he were standing there, she would have plunged it right into his heart. She was my father's age, and she had known my father for years. After my mother died, she wouldn't speak to him or even look at him.

I'd tell my father and stepmother I was going over to Rose's house, but they didn't care. Her place was only four blocks away; I'd roller skate over there and roller skate back. At 9 o'clock sharp after dinner, I'd put my roller skates on and I'd leave.

The reason I stopped going over there was that I went to work at age 12, and I was working nights, until 10 o'clock at night, six nights a week. The next time I saw her was at my wedding. I invited her.

The second Rose was also vaguely some kind of connection, possibly a cousin on my father's side. She was my Sunday Dinner Rose. She lived all the way in the Bronx. Every Sunday, she would make an elaborate meal, just for her and for me, because her husband was out working, and they didn't have any kids. After her dinner, I'd go to the park and hang out. She didn't care about hanging out with me; she just wanted to see me and cook for me. I traveled an hour and half to get to her in the Bronx and of course an hour and a half back. This wasn't a problem for me because, as I said, I knew the entire subway system at 10 years old. I'd go everywhere with confidence, anywhere I wanted to go. I'd ask questions like an adult if I didn't know.

The pain that I was in from living in that house was 25% less because of these regular visits to these two Roses. They took about 25% of the unpleasantness of the situation away, and that's a lot. I never missed a Tuesday, I never missed a Thursday, and I never missed a Sunday. If I saw that there was a movie playing, while on the train going up to the Bronx, Sunday Dinner Rose would give me the money so that I could go see it on my way back home instead of going to the park to hang out after dinner.

These were pleasant experiences out of a very unpleasant situation, three times a week for two years. That's a big, big plus. But once I went to work at age 12, it all went away. I don't know why I stopped seeing Sunday Dinner Rose, but thinking about it, there was something unpleasant that happened, and I think it was because she got sick and just couldn't do it anymore. She was a sickly woman the whole time I knew her. The fact that she wasn't at my wedding tells me she was probably gone by the time I got married eight years later at age 20. Otherwise, she would have been there; I would have invited her too.

These Roses gave me a feeling of family. They gave me three respites a week from a never-ending cycle of negativity. It's both easy and not easy to ride the subway three hours a day on a Sunday. But I used to stay in the first car and look out the window, and I used to see what the motor man would see. I'd be right next to his cabin to avoid the boredom of a ride like that, but it was worth it.

Inside That House

Inside that house, I found myself once again living with people who don't talk to you. They literally *do not* talk to you. They would set down rules, like if you aren't home by a certain time you'd be locked out. These were really *her* rules, but he looked the other way. That famous breakfast I always talk about: the cornflakes with the milk in it, prepared the night before, with a plate over it, out on the table all night, not in the refrigerator. That was my breakfast seven days a week. And if I didn't eat it, I'd have nothing to eat. For six straight years, "breakfast" was put in the dish the night before, with milk, covered with another dish, and left on the table. And we were fortunate enough at that time to *have* a refrigerator. To this day I never eat cold cereal. And again, if I didn't eat it, I had no breakfast. Was it spoiled? No. Was it horrible? Yes. I think she did that because it was easier for her.

[Why didn't you make your own breakfast?]

Because I did nothing. I was like a zombie—no resistance. No resistance—whatever she came up with, I took it. The only resistance I had was when I was somewhere between 15 and 16. She finally got to me one day. I literally was going to punch her out. She got to me. I started to approach her. My fist was balled up. I said to myself, "When you hit her, smack her right in the center of her face," because she really got to me for the first time in all these years. But fortunately I got the thought, "What is going to happen to me if I do this?" I thought of myself. Where that came from, how I had room for a rational thought, I don't know, but once I had the thought, I opened my fist and turned around and walked right out of the house.

I could have killed her, the way I felt. They abused the hell out of me the whole time, the whole six years. And he never said a word, *never*. He knew everything she was doing, and he never said a word.

To give you a picture of my father's narcissism: He's got a son, in a world war. Harry is away, overseas for more than four years, in the Pacific fighting the Japanese. Harry and I are writing to each other two to three times a week. (As an aside, just for some history, the mail was censored by the government, both ways.) He sees me writing these letters, and he knows who I'm writing to—this is his *firstborn*—not one time did he ever ask, "How's Harry doing?" or "What's going on?" This is a degree of narcissism where there's only one person in the world who matters—and that's *him*.

But I found a way to move forward in school, and I did. The only thing left that was positive was my ability not to get left back, and I did it, even though I was working six hours a day by the age of 12. I worked from 3 to 6 PM and again from 7 to 10 PM at the pharmacy. The whole reason I worked is that my parents refused to give me allowance. All the other kids got allowance, but I didn't, so that's the only way I could get my hands on any money. How could I have done my homework if I was working until 10 o'clock? And how did I get home by 10 o'clock when my stepmother would lock me out if I was home a second after 10?

I asked if I could leave five minutes early if I gave my boss back the five minutes, and that's how I got around that one. And I always had a girlfriend, and I'd ask her, "When you get your homework, could you make some notes and do a little side work for me?" In the morning, in homeroom, we had a half hour, and in that half hour I could whip up a little homework. And it worked. If I lost my girlfriend, I got another girlfriend who would do this same thing for me, and it worked. I said to them, "Just cover the homework. I have a half hour: if you do it properly, I'll figure it out." And I did this 7th grade and all through high school, and it worked. My brain *had* to have been working, because I had this motivation not to get left back, and this put my brain to work.

But I was so angry at school itself. Sometime after that horrible, horrible night—when my father broke up the family—for some reason, the teacher called me up to her desk. She said, "I know your mother just died..." But I was so embarrassed. I could feel 30 eyes staring at me, and I became so filled with anger at school from that point on, that there were many times where I took those 10-point tests, and knew all 10 answers, and I would leave three of them blank just so that I could get a 70% passing mark. I would know all 10, but I'd have no part of it. I didn't care. I did this from 7th grade until the age of 16. I managed to average 65-70% during those years.

I don't know if it was just general anger at the world, but I was really angry at the school. I remember in 8th grade, the assistant principal called me up to his office. He said, "I have your records, and I can tell something is very, very,

very wrong. I am looking at your early years and I'm looking at you now, and I can tell something is wrong. If you have anything to talk to me about, I could talk to you now." I shrugged my shoulders and refused to answer him. He could tell he was getting nowhere with me, and his intervention led to nothing.

CHAPTER 10
Hitler Invades Poland

On September 1, 1939, I'm on the playground and I'm playing paddle tennis, and I'm 11 years old. One of the bigger kids comes flying down the street, yelling, "Hitler just marched into Poland!!" I remember my reaction, because I was already interested in the subject, and I knew this was a major, major thing, and it's one that captured my attention throughout the war. We got the *Daily News* and the *Daily Mirror* delivered to the house every day, and I watched the progression of the war by following it closely, reading the papers. It was a matter of a young kid with a real interest in the war. It didn't affect any of my friends. They never talked about the war. This was a personal interest for me, and I stayed interested in it for the next five years. I learned the names, the mountains, the rivers, I did better with that than I did with my schoolwork. Had it been a subject, I would have gotten an A+. I even knew about the little war between Russian and Finland right before World War II. Nobody knows about this war. It was very interesting because it was in the winter. Finland is even colder and more bitter than Russia is in the winter. America was routing for Finland. But when spring came, Russia prevailed.

I just missed the draft. Just shy of my eighteenth birthday, Truman ended the draft. There wasn't even a hint that he was going to do this. Everyone was shocked. The war was over, and this was supposed to be the peacetime solders replacing the combat soldiers. They were called the Occupation Army. We occupied Germany, Japan, and Korea. The war ended August 7, 1945, but the draft continued until around May 15, 1946, when it abruptly ended. I turned 18 on June 9, 1946.

I was prepared to go overseas. We were a group of 12 friends, and 10 of them were in already, but I was the youngest of the group. One was in Germany, one was in the Philippines... I was ready to go. I could have had the experience of being in another country like my friends had, being in a foreign country for a year. It would have been a once-in-a lifetime experience. Or I might have liked living in Alabama or wherever. I had nothing in New York. I had nobody at home. I went from zero to being out in the world. In retrospect, I would have welcomed the experience, imagining what it could have been like for someone like me.

But the war ended on August 7, 1945, and I was living with my brother on the Lower East Side at the time. It was a Sunday, about 4 in the afternoon, and I heard a tumult going on outside, and there were throngs of people on the street and in the gutter. I was alone with my two baby nieces, and my brother and his wife were out— who knows where; they were always out partying—and there were kegs of beer out on the street, and I yelled down (I was only one fight up) and I wanted to know what was going on. And this lady said, "Japan surrendered! The war is over! Come down and have a drink!"

And I went downstairs, and the lady is there waiting for me, and she gives me a glass of beer, and she gives me a second glass of beer, and within 10 minutes I was drunk—I had never drunk alcohol before. I was only 17 years old, and I started arguing with the people, the revelers, and I said, "You can't keep reveling like this, because my nieces are trying to sleep and you're going to wake them up!" And I almost got violent, telling them, "You have to stop the yelling!"

What came out of that incident was that I never drank again. Because I was totally out of control, drunk. And I didn't like it. I never touched liquor after that. I'll never forget what it was like to be out of control of my mind.

CHAPTER 11
How I Got By Without Allowance

My First Dime

One day when I was 11 years old, I was walking down the street and the owner of a mom and pop store that sold only fruit and vegetables asked me if wanted to make some money. There were no horses and carts carrying fruits and vegetables up and down the street—this was Bensonhurst, not the Lower East Side, and besides, with the war going on, the horses were starting to die out anyway.

But mom and pop stores were very popular then. I said, "What do I have to do?" He had a list of addresses, and he said he had bags of produce that needed to be delivered around the neighborhood. I was the only kid in the neighborhood who didn't get allowance, so I was very excited about the prospect of making money. So I delivered four or five bags of produce for him that day, and when I was finished, he gave me a dime, and I flipped out. My mind was in *pennies*, not dimes. I was really hooked. I was so hooked after earning that dime that I wound up giving up my schoolyard baseball, everything, just so I could keep making money. So the owner told me to keep stopping by, and he was able to use me, and that was the beginning of my work career. This was the summer of 1939.

The Pharmacy

The pharmacy was my first real job in that I made a steady income of $3 a week for two years. I got this job because the kid that was working there was going to St. John's University to study to become a pharmacist, and he was later drafted, so they needed someone to fill in for him. I started this job at around 11 or 12 years old, working six days a week, six hours a day. I had to deliver medications door to door, stock the shelves—I did everything except run the register.

One of my many responsibilities at the pharmacy was writing the American Express money orders for the neighborhood, since there were no checking accounts in those days. If someone had to pay a bill, they would come to me, and I'd write an American Express money order for the gas company, or any kind of bill that they needed a money order for, and I'd do that from 7 to 10 o'clock at night. They would pay a nickel or a dime, according to the amount of the money order. I wrote a lot of money orders, because there was no other way for people to pay their bills.

In my mind, I was irreplaceable there. I answered all the phones; nobody had their own private phones because of the war. If you wanted to talk to someone, you'd call either the candy store or the pharmacist, and some kid would run up to go get the person out of the apartment to answer the phone. The kids would hang around and race to see who would get the person first, because they all wanted to get tipped a nickel for being the first. Anyway, I had multiple jobs there in the pharmacy, whereas the pharmacist had only one job: filling medications. I felt very important there.

When I first went to work there for the old pharmacist, I was working there for a year and a half, and we got along, and everything was fine. Then the old man hired a new pharmacist, and for whatever reason, he and I didn't care for each other at all. His name was Gradstein. I wasn't used to being treated the way he was treating me. Before he came along, I used to do whatever I wanted, but this guy kept watching me and giving me a hard time.

One night, Gradstein said to me, "There's a girl walking back and forth outside in front of the window. Why is she walking back and forth like that?" It was 9 PM, and I knew who she was. Her name was Shirley Rittenstein. She was waiting for me to get off work. So I said, "I don't know who she is. The sidewalk belongs to the city. Why don't you ask her?" He didn't like my answer. I had to work with this guy 20 hours a week. I don't like him, and he don't like me, and things were coming to a head. So that's what prompted me to go to the big boss with my ultimatum.

I told him, "We need to have very serious, private talk." I was very, very friendly with the boss, and I leveled with him. I told him, "I'm not getting along with Gradstein. He bothers me, he's watching me, and he won't let me do my work. I'm not used to this. I'm used to Moskowitz." I didn't threaten to leave, but as the conversation kept going, I said, "I'm not happy here, this is a great job, and everything is good, but he's spoiling it for me, and I can't keep working here as long as he's here. You have two options: either he goes, or I go." Meanwhile I'm only just barely 14 years old. But I was all business.

So the old guy gets really serious. His face turns pensive, and he starts rubbing his chin, deep in thought. I'm sitting there waiting for an answer, fully expecting he's going to side with me, because I do stuff in that store that nobody else does.

A good deal of time went by, and after he gave it a lot of thought, he finally spoke. "I'm thinking this over very carefully," he said, "and I've come to a decision. You were good enough to give me two options, so I'm going to give you two options also. Your two options are: either you get the hell out here tonight, or you get the hell out of here by the end of the week."

I was in *absolute shock*, but I chose to finish through the end of the week. It was good that I chose the second of the two options, because it gave me enough time to find another job, and I found one at the grocery store right around the corner. I always had a job.

The Grocer and the Tailor

The grocery store was a hard job, because I had to get up very early and get to the bakery by 5 o'clock in the morning in order to pick up the small and large rolls to bring them to the grocery store. I then had to deliver milk to people's houses by around 6, and while there I'd collect the empties and bring them back to the store. I had to do all of this before school started. I made very good money, double what I had been making at the pharmacy. So I was there before school, went to school, and then worked there after school until about 6 PM: double the money and fewer hours. But it came to an end when the store owner, a young widow—an angry, nasty woman—kept talking to me in a way that I could not accept. I was too sensitive. The tailor next door knew about her, and he told me one day, "If it doesn't work out here, you can come work for me," and that's when I quit on the spot and went to work for him.

Weekly Trips to Broadway

I was making enough money by this point that I was able to go to Broadway every week, on Sundays, to see the matinee shows, which of course were cheaper than the evening shows. The matinee shows were $1.20; I was way up in the balcony, but that was alright with me. It was very important for me to wear the best clothes I had for these shows, so I put together the following outfit, based on my own fashion sense.

It was a suit, forest green, and in my fashion mind, I needed brown suede shoes to go with that suit. Everything had to match in my head. I'd have the suede shoes, and I'd have the forest green suit, and the shirt had to be a dark green corduroy, wide wale, heavy material. And that was the picture I had in my head of what I wanted to be wearing, so I put that outfit together and that's what I wore to the Broadway shows every week.

I went every week for a while, and this went on from age 13 to age 15, so I must have seen a lot more than 100 shows. In fact, I was so into these Broadway shows that this is where I took Grandma on our first date, on a Saturday night. We went to see *Anna Lucasta*, on Broadway, which was memorable because it featured an all-black cast. This was January 1945. Everyone else would have taken their first date to the movies, but not me: it had to be Broadway.

But before I started dating Grandma, my best friend, Harold ("Heshie"; I was "Sef" or "Seffie"—nobody ever called each other by their legal names), who was also the best man at my wedding, asked me where I go every Sunday, all dressed up. I told him where I go and what I do, and he said, "Maybe I can go with you?"

July 4th 1945

So I told him, "You can go with me only on one condition. You have to be dressed for it. You have to get dressed up; you can't go in your schoolyard clothes." He ended up going with me for at least a year, and he loved it. We'd see a show, and then we'd go to the famous automat Horn & Hardart, and I'd have the same thing every week: baked beans with strips of bacon on top. Sometimes I had two of them. That's all I ate there. After the automat, we'd go to Central Park, and we rent a rowboat for 35 cents an hour. I did the rowing; Heshie was my passenger. He never missed going out on Sundays. He loved them as much as I did.

To give you a deeper idea of my thing for Broadway, on Wednesdays, during the second half of my last year of school before I dropped out, I'd slip out of school at about 9 in the morning, and I'd run to the nearest train station, to Times Square, and I'd go to the Paramount for 45 cents. I did this every week, and I'd still get back in time for my after-school job. That's how much I loved going to the shows. I got away with this by ripping up the Delaney card[3] when they handed it to me. So as far as anyone was concerned, I wasn't even there.

---

[3] Delaney cards were used in the New York City public school system to keep attendance records.

CHAPTER 12
Growing Up and Moving Out

I stayed in that household until I was 16 so that I could finish school, all the while planning to drop out. The kids in the neighborhood by this point were only getting a buck allowance while I was making $3 a week. I was really independent by 13 years old. I could do anything I wanted, I could spend anything I wanted, because I didn't get any allowance. I had my own money. I grew up; I matured. I was growing up light years faster than my peers by this point.

As far as my friends went, it was very, very important to me that nobody knew my story. When you're a kid, you want to be like every other kid on the block. You don't want to be a freak. So you just don't talk about yourself, and you don't let anyone go to your house. *Ever.* As I said, I always had a girlfriend, and back then in those days you really only went a couple of months with that girl, even though you were in a group. I lived the same kids' life like all the other kids, with the ball playing and all the rest. I was like all the other kids in that respect. But they were not to know anything about my personal life. I worked very hard to guard that. I knew all the parents of the boys and the girls, so if one of my girlfriends said her mother wants to meet me, I would break up with that girl. Because I didn't want any questions, which would have been very, very common in that close-knit neighborhood. I wouldn't go to any of the houses of these girls and sit in their house and possibly answer their questions—*Who are your parents? Why don't we ever see them?*—and the only way I could avoid this was to break it off. I knew all of these parents from working in the pharmacy, and I didn't want to deal with it. My private life was a secret.

I worked in the pharmacy 1941 and 1942, and I had to deliver medications to sick people all over the neighborhood, cough medicine and stuff like that—people who were homebound and so forth. All the fathers were working, so there was very little male contact, but there was very heavy contact with the mothers.

The War Effort

After Pearl Harbor, the government came into our pharmacy and asked if we could collect any kind of metal for the war effort. This was my particular job, about three times per week. I would put down a carton—not large, not small—and I'd put a note in there that said, "Please return all your materials that contain metal for the war effort." In my little neighborhood, I would fill up three cartons a week: toothpaste tubes, anything that had any metal in it. The government would come around and pick up the cartons every week, and it was all for arms for the military. The neighborhood people were so into this, it was so important to them, that they would check the house before they went to the pharmacy, and they would look around to collect anything with metal. They would always come in with something. Not like today, where nobody cares about anything.

Every eight weeks the local Red Cross would come in as well, and I always donated blood. I did that from 16 to 18 years old on West 40th Street in Manhattan, and they would take a pint of blood from me each time. I was so devoted to this that I ended up getting a pin from the government called a Two Gallon Pin, because of how much blood I donated to the government. My blood donations were especially valuable to them because I learned back then that I have a rare blood type, B-, and only 5% of the population has it. The only thing that stopped me from giving blood was that the war ended. All I could think of was just that injured soldier bleeding to death—not humanity as a *whole*. It was just that one pint of blood and that one soldier that I was thinking about. They said my blood was turned into plasma, and that plasma was sent over to the battlefield.

I was at one point contacted by the National Rare Blood Club, and I was asked to join. And one of the benefits of joining was that I and even my whole family would be entitled to blood if we ever needed it. And as a rare-blood person, it's possible I may need it in the future. I *need* that B- blood. So I joined that club in my 20s, and I've belonged to that club since forever.

The other thing everyone did for the war effort was food rationing. We had to control the food supply to support the military. Since they didn't ration the military, they had to ration the public, so certain items were limited. Families were issued a booklet of food stamps once every three months. You had to use up all the stamps by the expiration date. For example, you were limited to about a quarter of a pound of butter per week. Even shoes were rationed. You could only get two pairs of shoes a year. Handling the food stamps was a big part of my job in the grocery store. You didn't need them in the pharmacy, because there weren't many products in the pharmacy that applied to these stamps, but in the grocery stores, a lot of things were limited and restricted. Even gas was restricted. People were only allowed to use six gallons of gas a week, for example, and this took a heavy toll on people. Everyone had these food stamps. You couldn't go food shopping without them. The food rationing stopped when the war stopped.

Dropping out with Vic Damone on my Birthday

I quit school on my sixteenth birthday. My stepmother had to go to the school to sign the papers to get me out of there, so I had no choice but to approach her. I told her, "I'm quitting school today." So she said, "I'm busy today." So I said, "Then I'll tell them that my mother has things to do. They'll come after you, but I don't care. I'm leaving whether you go or you don't." I said to myself, "I'm *going* because this is my last day of school. I'm finished with school for good." So she got scared and she went with me. She signed the papers, and I never even went home after that. I went straight to my brother Sidney's house and I never went back to that dark place again. I only had a few things with me in a paper bag.

Only two kids dropped out of Lafayette High School on that Friday, June 9, 1944: me and the famous Vic Damone. His real name was actually Vito Farinola, and his reasons for dropping out were a lot different from mine. His reason was that he was helping the family financially because the father could not work anymore, and he felt that his music lessons were the least important of the family expenses, so he got this part-time job as an usher in the Paramount Building while also trying to finish school. The Paramount Theater was on the street level, and it was a twelve-story building. So he was working this part time job while he was in school, but he decided he wanted to work full time and stop the lessons. His mother said that they'll find a way, but that he *can't* stop those lessons. That led to his dropping out and moving to full-time work, and that's when he met Perry Como in the elevator.

These performers, many times they would stay in the Paramount Building and they'd do three, four shows a day, so they hung around in the building. And so by chance, Como was in the elevator with Vito, and they were alone, and Vito stopped the elevator in between floors. And he said, "Mr. Como, I have something to ask you. Is it okay if I ask you a question?" He then briefly explained his family situation, and he said, "I feel guilty paying that vocal teacher because the family needs the money, but my mother said I can't stop because I'm too good. Could I sing a couple of notes for you, and could you give me your honest opinion of my voice?" Como agreed, and Vito sang "I Have But One Heart"—it starts out in English and then it switches to Italian. And Como said, "If there's any way you can continue, you should, because you're good. Keep going."

And from that point on, once he had Perry Como's positive opinion on the matter, he stopped feeling guilty about it and he kept going. And he ended up becoming Vic Damone, the famous singer and actor. He started out singing in a nightclub in Manhattan where new talent would be booked, and from there he made it big in a very short time. He ended up naming his first and only son Perry. And the funny thing is that sometime in the late 1990s, possibly around 2000, I got a note from Vic (when your husband at the time was playing in a band with Vic Damone as the feature singer), and the note said: "To Art, Best Regards, Vic Damone." I can't say for sure if he remembered me or not, but I definitely remember him. I remember talking with him very briefly while his mother and my stepmother were signing us out for good. I never knew him in school, because I wasn't in any of his classes. This was the first and last time I had ever met him.

CHAPTER 13
A Giant Mistake

After dropping out of school I went straight to my brother Sidney's house, not having any idea what I was getting myself into. I found myself at 16 years old walking into this babysitting situation, three to four days a week, while my brother and his wife are out until 3, 4 o'clock in the morning, and I had to go to work the next day. This was another cold water flat—no heat, no hot water. And I didn't have to deal with any of that where I came from in Bensonhurst, though I certainly had memories of what it was like. There's *nothing* colder than being indoors in the cold months with no heat and no hot water. My sister-in-law and brother and the babies all slept in one room with a kerosene heater, but that didn't warm all the other rooms. And I remember many nights sleeping in the freezing cold, in all my clothes, and in my coat. But I didn't get sick. I was healthy as an ox.

My brother had his own business, so he could sleep in and party all night. And you'd think he could afford to live in better living conditions. But there was no building happening starting with

Pearl Harbor. All construction stopped, so there was no available housing. Even if you lived in terrible living conditions, by 1944 everything came to a halt, and there was no place to go. It was horrible. And we had rats, too. I watched my brother chase a rat inside the apartment.

Moving away from the two people I hated had many advantages, but it had many disadvantages too. If I had to do it all over again, I'd have to say no, I wouldn't have left when I did. If I had stuck it out there for another year, I would have waited for my seventeenth birthday, and I would have enlisted. I wouldn't have thought about getting killed. You don't think of things like this when you're 17. Maybe I would have started another life somewhere else, gotten to meet new people, see new things. It would have given me a reason not to come back to New York at all. Maybe I could have built another life in another place.

But I found myself in this freezing cold apartment taking care of two babies at the age of 16. And while I was there, after six months of being there in the apartment, my brother was drafted. He was gone eight months, sent to an army camp in

Georgia. When he was drafted, he told me that when he leaves, his business is going to fold if something isn't done. So he sat me down and told me exactly what I had to do.

Meanwhile I already had a job: I was learning how to be a cutter in the garment district. My brother Harry had gotten me the job from 5,000 miles away. (He was serving in the Pacific, but he knew people.) So first Harry got me this job, and now my other brother Sidney is telling me I have to take on this additional responsibility. I said, "How am I supposed to eat lunch?" He had no answer for that. He just said, "When you get paid, you give all your money to Shirley." So I'm thinking, "I don't get paid, and I don't get to eat lunch either."

I don't know what he would have said if I had said no, but I felt like I had no choice. I knew I was in a trap, and I had no alternative. And he knew it too. Harry is gone, my father's gone. This is the only place left, so he had me in that trap. I just agreed to do it because I had no place else to go.

This is how I did it. On my way back to work I'd have a hot dog, and then I'd have to go from one location to another within the garment district. I had to make about three or four different stops within one hour ... and I did it. I did everything he said to do. I made it work, and I gave his wife all the money when I got paid. And when he came home after serving for eight months—he was discharged on a mental discharge, because he was considered mentally ill under Section 8—I expected that he was going to pay me *something* for those eight months when I was keeping his business afloat, but he didn't pay me anything. And I was contributing something like $15 a week to the household. So he had a fantastic deal with me.

Thinking back, I was still happy at the time that I had made that move. It was only years later that I said to myself, "I should have stayed where I was." I made that move impulsively. I turned 16, left school, moved out, and got a job all on the same day. Another negative was that every single night, when they didn't go out, I went back to the old neighborhood to see my old friends. I made no friends in the new neighborhood except for a neighbor. So every night that I was free, I went back to the old neighborhood and hung out with my old friends. Maybe about three to four times a week I went back, no matter the weather, and it took me an hour to get there and an hour to get back. And I still had to go to work the next day.

CHAPTER 14
How I Met Grandma

My second home was the candy store, no matter what the weather was, all year round. It was my home away from home. The owners had a relative who came to visit them, and she was Grandma's next door neighbor. Her name was Sarah Lustig. One day we were sitting at a booth, and she said, "I want to have a talk with you." I said, "Ten minutes," because I had a softball game. She said, "There's a girl who lives next door to me, about your age, and you would make such a good couple." I said, "I have 25 girlfriends, so why do I need to?"

But she saw that Grandma was messed up, and she was trying to save Grandma ... and she saw something in me. She really cared about Rita. She loved her. She had more feelings for her than her own mother did.

It killed her to see how they were treating Rita. She saw everything that was going on, and she wanted to find a way for Rita to get away from them. She saw in me someone who could make that happen, so she just would not stop trying to get the two of us together. She was very persistent.

Grandma's parents *hated* Sarah for matching Grandma up with me. Rae and Joe never approved of me because I didn't have something to offer them that would make them look good. I didn't have a trade or anything much going on at the time that I met Grandma.

But anyway Sarah came to the store every Saturday, and every Saturday she would bring up Rita. One day I finally decided to meet her. I thought maybe it would be interesting and exciting to meet someone new. And besides, my curiosity had gotten the better of me after four or five weeks of Sarah bringing it up. So I finally said, "I'll do it; give me the address."

She came back the following week and told me that Rae said Rita can't go out with a boy alone, and that she'll let her go only if he brings a friend—and then Rita will bring a friend. So *two couples* would be allowed.

I went over to the schoolyard and told all the guys I'm going on a blind date, and that I needed to bring one of them with me so I could go on this date. I saw it as adventure, but the guys were all incredulous. They all said, "Where does she live?" I said, "In Brooklyn," but I was holding back telling them how far away she actually lived—Kosciuszko Street. One of the kids said, "But that's in *Poland*!" So I told the kid, "You can't come with me because you're too stupid! It's in Brooklyn, not Poland!" I'll never forget that.

But one of them I was finally able to convince to go: Stanley Arkin. Rita brought Renee. I told Stanley I thought Rita was "okay" after that blind date, and Stanley said, "You mean we're not coming back anymore?" Because he was *crazy* about Renee. I kept coming back for his sake. I wasn't crazy about Grandma, not the way Stanley was crazy about Renee. All the next many dates after that were for Stanley. But after a while, week after week after week, I started to warm up to Grandma.

Grandma was head over heels for me from day one. She said she thought she died and went to heaven when she first saw me, but I didn't feel the same way at the time. But after getting to know her, one month going into the second month and so on ... by the time we went to Prospect Park on Easter Sunday, I was really starting to get close to Grandma.

Easter Sunday 1945

By then, she knew everything about me, but I didn't know what she had gone through...yet. I didn't know about that difficult childhood she had. That story unfolded a couple of months later. I'd say by about the four-month mark, we became really close, and by then, Stanley and Renee broke up.

After sixteen dates, Grandma Rae knew me and trusted me enough to go out with Rita alone. And we were off on our own. The strange thing is that Grandma Rita was one of a group of five girls all joined at the hip; they were always together, though Rita mostly just tagged along with them. Flashing forward, two others in my group of friends—the same group on that playground when I was preparing to go on that blind date with Grandma—wound up marrying two of the girls in Rita's friend group: they eventually came on dates and later got married.

All the time I lived with my brother I was dating Grandma. He moved after 1944 to a beautiful house in Brooklyn (he got a loan from the government). So we moved in 1944, and I started dating Grandma in 1945. It took three-quarters of an hour by trolley car to get from his new house in East Flatbush to where Grandma lived in Brooklyn—Kosciuszko street in Bedford Stuyvesant. I was also working the entire time I was dating Grandma. She was still in school.

One Saturday night, Grandma and I were out on a date in Times Square. It was February 1946; I was 17 years old, and Grandma was 16. I told her that I had signed the initial enlistment paper—now, meanwhile, remember, her brother Theodore had just died in the war—and when I told her this she was absolutely distraught. She asked me why I'd want to do that, and I told her, "I'm nowhere, I have no trade, so let me start my life six months earlier so I could get out at 19½ instead of 20." But Grandma pleaded with me not to sign the final papers.

I remember I got the call from Shirley, my brother Sid's wife, that there were two MPs [military police officers] at her door; they were there for the second and final signature that would have made my enlistment official. I told her to tell them I changed my mind, and that I'm just going to wait until I'm drafted.

March comes, then April comes, and in the middle of April, on a Saturday, I'm on my way to the schoolyard to play baseball, and I get to the corner of the block, where the newsstand was, and in big bold letters there's a headline on all the newspapers:

TRUMAN ENDS DRAFT

There was no notice or anything; he just ended it on the spot, two months before my eighteenth birthday. I don't know what would have happened to Grandma if I had gone overseas or even to some military base somewhere else in the U.S. and had left her with those two animals for parents.

We continued to date, and I took Grandma to her prom. I looked out for her while she was finishing up her high school years, almost as though I were in a parental role.

I remember an incident when she was

in her senior year in high school. She ran into some kind of a problem where the school said they had to talk to her parents in person or she wouldn't be able to graduate. I don't remember what the issue was. But I remember I told her, "Don't say anything to your parents. I'm going to call the school and I'm going to tell them I'm your father." I mixed in a little European the way the Europeans would speak English. I recited for a while what I was going to say, and when I had it down pat, I called the school, and I gave them a whole story about why I can't come into the school to talk to them, because I can't close the barber shop, and we solved the whole problem right there on the phone. The example of this chutzpah that I had is just to show that I did what I had to do to survive. In simple language, I had to enter the adult world very early. If I had stayed in the mentality of a little kid, I'd be dead. My only Achilles heel was my brothers. Only my brothers were able to get through and trick me. They were eight and twelve years older than me, and I looked up to them. And they were able to get over on me. I couldn't refuse anything they wanted.

But with Grandma it was different compared to any of my other relationships. I took care of her; I helped her find her first job out of high school—office work—and we ended up getting married when she was 19 and I was 20. But to this day I still can't help but wonder what it would have been like if I had just enlisted.

CHAPTER 15
The Birth of the NBA

From January 1945 through all of 1946, dates were usually a movie, because every week there were new movies, followed by dinner at a restaurant. It could have been in Times Square or in downtown Brooklyn, which is like a mini Times Square, and it was always a double date. Rae said Grandma couldn't go out with some strange boy, so we had to double date, but we ended up *liking* going double dating, and we did this for two years.

Toward the end of 1946, possibly around November, the first game ever of the BAA—the Basketball Association of America, which was the precursor to the NBA—took place, and we were there, on one of our dates.

There's a side story to this. It's not a short story, but it's a very important story. College basketball in those years was so huge and so popular that at the beginning of the season you couldn't get any tickets for any of the double headers. They were at Madison Square Garden, which held 18,000 people. Two New York colleges played two out-of-state schools, two games in one night, and there were 32 of these double-header games in a season. The reason I went to every single game was because a very close friend of mine, who went to NYU, was able to give me the cheap seat in the nosebleed section. There were basketball games going on three days a week. I went to every game, and I took Grandma every Saturday. But that's not the side story.

The New York Knickerbockers are ready to open up the season with a brand new league, a professional league, but they can't find a place to play. So they decide on renting a space in a regiment armory on Lexington or Madison Avenue and 26th Street. It was the home of our National Guard. This was in 1946. You paid $1 per person, and you got a folding chair and a program. You could walk around and decide where you wanted to sit. The armory only held a fraction of what the Garden held, but once the BAA was formed, Grandma and I stopped going to the Garden and we attended all of the BAA games on Saturdays.

After the game was over, we'd walk up to the theater district and we'd have dinner in Times

Square—walked from 26th Street up to about 44th Street. We weren't eating until around 10 at night, and we wouldn't get home until 1 or 2 o'clock in the morning. But I still got up the next morning and played stickball on Sunday mornings. I was an athlete.

In 1951 one of the biggest scandals in sports history happened. A couple of college basketball players got caught up in it, and it was such a scandal that the country all but gave up on college basketball for about ten years. There was a lot of gambling that went on in college basketball games. In 1951, some gangsters got to these kids and told them to shave points. They weren't told to lose, but they were told to stay under a certain number of points. This affected the betting of millions of people—there were millions and millions of dollars involved. And about half a dozen kids were caught. It damaged college basketball for the next ten years.

But what happened? Now the Knicks had a place to play, and they moved into Madison Square Garden in 1951, and they're still there. That's the side story. The only ones who benefitted was the Knicks. College basketball moved from a giant sport to a tiny sport. The teams moved back to playing in their schools. Professional basketball picked up their fans little by little. The BAA had already merged with the NBL in 1949, but by 1951 with college basketball's scandal, the NBA started to become really big.

Grandma wasn't really a fan of basketball. She just wanted to be wherever I was. But I stayed a real fan of basketball for decades, and I stayed loyal to the sport until these millionaire players started going down on one knee. That finished me off. I never watched it after that.

CHAPTER 16
From My Brother's House to a Place of My Own

I was with my brother for years, from 1944 into 1948—all of these years overlapping my dating years with Grandma. Then came a nasty breakup with my brother when everything came to a head in 1948. Grandma Rae asked me who does my laundry. I told her, "My sister-in-law gives the laundry to the laundry company." There were dozens of laundry companies in the neighborhood at that time. I told her that I put my clothes in with the rest of the family's clothes, and then when I told her what I gave them—she was in shock. She told me that she pays less for laundry for the four of them in her house than my sister-in-law is taking from me.

I didn't confront Shirley, but this was a freak thing: On the day of that conversation with Rae, my brother Sid, Shirley's husband, for some reason had to call me. He called Rita's house to speak to me, and Rae happened to pick up the phone—and did she let him have it! This all happened on the same day. She *really* let him have it!

When I got on the phone, I remember what he said to me. He said, "You let a female run your life like this?" I said, "No comment, I don't want to talk about this." Shortly thereafter, Shirley said to me, "You can't have dinner here anymore unless you give us more money." I said, "I can't give you any more money, so forget it. I'll just eat out." So for the next six months or so, I'd have a hamburger and French fries every night, but it was already strained there anyway.

Shirley was Sid's student. He assigned her to do all of his dirty work. So he'd dispatch her to extract money from me. One day many years later, Sid's son called me and said he wanted me to tell him what his father was like, but I told him he's better off not knowing. Sid was a clone of my father. Both of them were severe narcissists. It's a mystery how someone like Terri, Sid's second wife, who was an angel, put up with him. There was a 13-year age difference between Terri and Sid. She was his secretary and they ended up getting married, but they couldn't have been more different. She told me once, many years later, "I'll never forget the first night I met you." This was before Sid and Terri got married. They came to Sunnyside for dinner with me and

Grandma, and Terri said she was so nervous. "But within a few minutes, you made me feel so comfortable," she said. And then she said, "I fell in love with you that night, but what could I do? I met Sid already!" It cracked me up, but I just left it alone.

One day in the beginning of 1948, Rae said to me, "There's a furnished room across the street, and I know the owners of the house. Why don't you take that room, and you'll live there, and you'll have dinner here every night." It was $15 a week for the room, and that's what I did. Grandma and I were together and all but engaged by this point, so that's what I did. The entire 1948 I lived in that room and had dinner across the street at Rita's mothers house. And I was glad to be out of my brother's house, because it was so strained.

My brother was a user. Remember *Dear Abby?* The writer of the column once gave this advice: there are two types of people that make up our world, users and usees. And the users are awesome at how they can pick out their victims, the usees. My brother was a user, and I was his usee. He took whatever he could get out of me. I was out of the frying pan and into the fire by going to him. And the fire is much hotter than the frying pan.

On January 1, 1949, I married Grandma, but we had no place to live. So we lived in that furnished apartment across the street from her mother's house, and we slept there and ate at Rae's house every night. And we lived there like that for a year and two months until we finally found an apartment.

You still couldn't get an apartment at that time, so I had to slip $700 under the table to the super for a beautiful apartment in Sunnyside, Queens—elevator and everything. I had to borrow the money to bribe the super to get this apartment for me. The supers made out like crazy at that time.

But even after all that, I did stay in contact with my brother Sidney because his was the only "family" I had. If I had to do it over again though, I wouldn't have bothered. But I was too fragile at the time.

CHAPTER 17
A Rescue Marriage

The wedding was an elaborate affair of 150 people. Grandma and I didn't want it, and we told her mother Rae, but Rae said we have to have it, and there was no negotiating it. Grandma's parents paid for all of it. I told them I could really, really use some of that money to help me out because I was struggling; our two salaries combined were crap. I really could have used some of the money that was going into this wedding, but she said we're *having* the wedding and that's it.

So I said, at least I don't want my father there, and I don't want my stepmother there. She said, "They have to come, because how would that look for the neighbors?" She lost me after that. I could never look at her again. Even my two brothers were there. But it was everything for "the neighbors." She didn't have a single iota of feeling or compassion for what I was going through, and she knew absolutely *everything* about what I had gone through. So she lost me. She lost me for life. The whole wedding was for the neighbors, because we didn't want it. The whole building was invited.

Out of the 150 people who attended, only 10 of them were mine. Heshie was my best man, and his parents were there, because they were very, very good to me, and I had one very distant relative, a single lady. But still, it was a beautiful wedding. Even over the years—20, 30, 40 years later—we would look at our wedding album and our feelings were still the same. All the bad feelings came back. The terrible feelings were never softened over time. Every single person in that album is gone. The only one still alive is me.

Rita needed rescuing, because she was drowning. I wasn't drowning. I was in a very difficult, difficult situation, but I never felt I was drowning. I was doing the best I could under the circumstances. I was able to work. I became an adult as a teenager and was able to be really tough—not *tough guy* tough—but in terms of surviving. But she was beaten, completely beaten from the day she was born. She was almost destroyed.

A rescue marriage is a psychological term that I got in counseling. And what I also got in counseling is that they almost never work out. They are doomed to failure. This is what the counselor told me in the back-and-forth one day. I came back to the counselor when she said, "They cannot work; they're doomed." So I said, "Why did mine work, then?"

She said, "Yours was special; it had something attached that the average rescue marriage doesn't have. She said if it had been just the two of you without the children, it wouldn't have lasted. But you had Sharon, and if you ever left that child, you'd become your father, and that was out the question for you. He threw you away, and you'd be throwing her away, and you could never do that. But otherwise, with just two adults, it can't work."

When you're together for many, many years—even after your kids are grown, and everything is basically okay—let's say you're together for 20 years, you stay together, and you finish out your life. But when you're younger and you're not fully mature yet, these marriages don't tend to stay together.

I met Grandma when I was 16 years old; she was 15. You're not the same at 25 as when you're 15. But at some point you become fully mature—let's say that by age 30, you are who you are. But I'll never forget something. I was 23 years old, and Grandma was 22, and there was something going on verbally between us, and I realized this: we're now together seven years, and I'm talking like a 23-year-old, and she's still talking like she's 15 years old. She never changed. And it hit me like a bomb. It was a very difficult night for me when I came to this realization.

Looking back now, Sharon was here, she was 1 year old, and she's here to say, and we're locked in, but if we hadn't had any children at that point, I really think I would have split. It was such a shock to me when I realized how far we had diverged from one another. Much later on, I learned about arrested development, and when I look back, that's exactly what I was looking at. At some point she just stopped her normal development. More or less she stayed 15 throughout the rest of our marriage. We had a lot of friends, but mostly all of our friends were mine. She had one true, lasting friend, Julie, who I'll talk about later, but she just hooked onto me and I ran everything.

A Psychopathic Mother

Grandma Rita definitely was not wanted. Her mother had already had three abortions, and she wasn't allowed to have any more. Even her brother Stuart wasn't wanted, but Stuart had a rebellious nature, and he fought his parents, Rae and Joe. Rita was passive; she couldn't fight the things they did to her. When it came to Rita's family, her mother poisoned the whole family. But Rae was especially hateful toward Rita, who was the only girl, because Rita was a *female*. Rae had a thing for males.

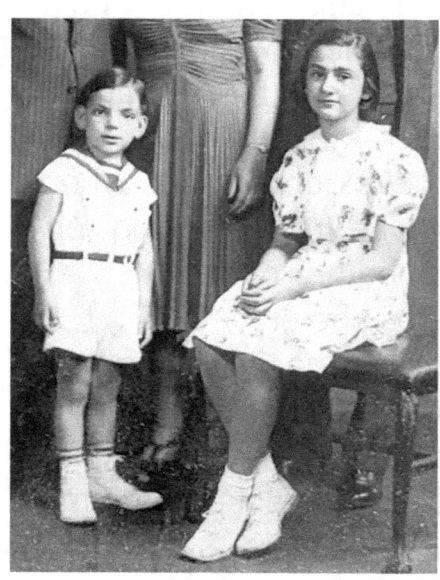

Before I met Rita, she was a selective mute. On top of that, she threw up in school every day. That's how bad her anxiety was, growing up in a house like this. People used to hang their clothes out to dry on clothes lines. That was Grandma's job, because Rae was always working. And Rita had to do this at 8, 9, 10 years old. Grandma told me that when she was hanging the clothes, she would find herself hoping, hoping, hoping she would fall out of the window. So she was really suicidal to get out of that house.

Rae was a psychopath. She had to be the best at everything and the most popular: the best cook, the best knitter, the best everything. And she really *was* the best cook. But she wouldn't let anyone take any of her food out of her house if there were leftovers after a gathering, no matter how much food was left over. If she allowed anyone to take any food home, they wouldn't be praising her in front of her, so everyone always had to eat in front of her, and they had to praise her, and she always had a ton of food left over.

Grandma Rita knew how to do all the same things, but by the time Rita was a teenager she was *better* than Rae at knitting, and the neighbors would praise her to Rae, who started to look at her own daughter as her rival. Rae became extremely jealous of Rita. One day Rae couldn't take it anymore, and when all the neighbors left, she turned to Rita and warned her, "Don't you *ever* do that again. You don't do anything without asking me!" Rae felt so threatened by Rita's talent. Rita was only 14 years old when she started creating such beautiful pieces with her knitting.

Every friend that Rae had, she had to manipulate. The ones who wanted no part of that would be with her once and would never come back. But the ones who could be manipulated came back, and they would be her victim. I'll give you an example with her own husband. Joe had a heart condition. She'd cook something that he was not supposed to eat, and then she'd entice him that he must taste it. But this was food he *really* was not supposed to eat. And she'd work on him, and work on him, and I'd sit there at the table and watch how she kept working him over until he caved, just so that he would praise her for her cooking.

With her friends she would do that too, all the time. Most of this was wrapped up with food and the kitchen table. The friends would come into the house and she would be so controlling. There was this one woman, and she said, "No, I can't eat that," and I'd watch Rae as she would nudge the food over on the table toward the woman, inch by inch, and when it got close enough, the woman couldn't resist. She took and ate the cake that she wasn't supposed to have.

Rae never tried her head games with me, but she used to gaslight Grandma constantly. I never saw it, because it happened in the earlier years, before I met Grandma, but Grandma told me the things she used to do. One thing Rae liked to do went something like this. She'd tell Grandma, "Put this over there on the table." So Grandma would put it there. Rae would then get angry and start insulting Grandma for putting it there. So Grandma would put it back where it was in the first place, and then she'd be berated for that, too. Nothing Grandma ever did was ever right. She was always being criticized and mocked; she would routinely be told that things that were happening were not happening. These mind games went on and on for so many years that they took away Grandma's ability to function.

Grandma was sexually molested over and over again by men in the building. When I asked her why she never told anyone, she said, "I didn't tell my mother, because if I told my mother I'd get slapped in my face and I'd be told, 'Stop lying! Don't lie to me like that!'" And I accepted what she was saying, because that's probably true. She wasn't safe in her apartment building. The men would grab her in the hallway. That's what would have happened. She had nobody to talk to. So that's part of the reason why she went silent. She would tell everyone, "I was born the night I met Arthur. I was born that night." And it's more than partly true. In fact, her actual emotional age was probably younger than 15. She became arrested long before she met me.

Rae did not like me from the beginning. I feel like the only reason they wanted me to marry Rita—after all, I was not a doctor or a lawyer or an Indian Chief—is because they were afraid Rita would become pregnant. I had been dating her for four years, and they'd be mortified if Rita got pregnant out of wedlock, so that's when Rae came up with her big idea.

We come back from a New Year's Eve party, and it's 4 o'clock in the morning, and there are ten people standing around in Rae's house. We walk in, and out of the blue she makes an announcement: "Next year we're having a wedding!" So Rita says, "Who's getting married?" and she says, "You two are getting married next year!" So Rita turns and says to me—note this is the *first* time marriage ever came up in all the years we were dating—"You want to get married?" And I said, "I don't care, you want to get married?" And that's how the proposal went. I said, "I don't care either way." Some proposal.. But Grandma didn't care either. We never even thought about marriage. We were having the time of our lives, going out three days a week and having a ball.

Rae was insane, and Rita's father Joe didn't give a damn about her. He was okay with the multiple abortions, and he didn't even want his sons either. He was a very, very, very weak man. Rae was the power. He felt nothing for Rita.

Rae adored one child—the oldest son Theodore, who was killed in the war. When the news came that he had been killed, the choice for the family was, you could leave the body in a cemetery in Europe or you could have the body shipped home and the government would pay for it. She wanted the body to come back home. They flew the body back, and they had the funeral, a few months after I met Grandma. Grandma wanted me at that funeral. I didn't want to go, but Grandma begged me to please go, and for her I went.

At the funeral, Rae was out of her mind with grief, and Grandma—and I watched this, I didn't move—when the mother was going berserk, Grandma went over to her mother to calm her down, and Grandma said—and I heard it—"You have two other children, and we need you, so calm down." And what did Rae do? She flung Grandma away from her; it wasn't just a little nudge or a push. She flung her away. It was an unbelievable memory. She didn't answer Grandma at all; she just flung her away.

If I had been a normal teenager, when I first started seeing Grandma, I would have seen a lot more of the red flags that went on in that house, but I didn't see much of it or notice it at the time, I didn't see the red flags—and they were all over the place—because I was so screwed up myself. I would have gone on one date and I would have been out the door, but I wasn't normal. It turned out to be a wonderful thing for me, because this was the first girlfriend I had that wasn't in my own neighborhood. I just wanted to be as "normal" as everyone else in my neighborhood, so it was fine to tell Grandma about my own experiences. I was glad to have someone I could talk to about them.

The More I See You

I had it rough, but nobody did to me the things that were done to her. And I cared for her enough to stay with her, and I stayed with her because I had nobody. It could have been anyone if I had met someone at 16, when I was completely alone in the world. It could have been Jane Doe. But this was the first time anyone ever depended on me, needed me. If I had met a strong or normal person, I don't know how that would have went. Grandma's dependency on me was an ego boost. It was the first time I ever had the feeling of "family" in having Grandma in my life, when she started to lean on me, and depend on me, and it gave me the first-ever feeling of what a family is like.

When I was 11 years old, they had just taken me out of foster care. I had homework, and I didn't want to do it in the house if I could come to my friend's house instead and do my homework with him. The friend's name was Jerome Walk. He said, "Yeah, you could. We could do it in the basement." So I'd go to his house, and I'd do my homework, and I'd get ready to go home. I did this four nights a week just so I didn't have to be in my house. And after a while, after about a month, his mother said to me, "Why don't you go out through the side door like the family does? You're like part of the family—use the side door."

And one night, when I was saying goodnight to her, she took me in her arms, and she held me so tight, and she said to me, "You're gonna be a heartbreaker." And I panicked! I didn't know what a heartbreaker was; I was only 11 years old. And I realized then that I had never had a hug before—from *anybody*. That was the first hug of my life. At 11 years old. And she's embedded in my brain, what she looked like and everything else. Here I am, 85 years later, talking about my friend's mother, who gave me a hug. And this was some hug for a first hug. Wow!

But Grandma was my entire family, and I was her entire family; we were all each other had.

Even though we saw each other every day, we would send each other these cards—beautiful, elaborate cards; mushy, mushy Valentine's cards, and the like. I was the first one to ever care about her; she was the first one to ever care about me.

Our song when we were dating, but one that really became our song for life, was "The More I See You," from a 1945 musical film called *Diamond Horseshoe*. I would sing this song to

Grandma, and it would make her so happy. We were on a big high during those dating years.

> *The more I see you...*
> *The more I want you..*
> *Somehow this feeling...*
> *Just grows and grows...*

Usually in these rescue marriages, when the real world sets in, you start missing those skewed highs. With Grandma and me, Friday and Saturday dating was everything. But when the couple gets married and the problems set in, you don't have any way to deal with it, and I understood clearly what the therapist was telling me. Those marriages keep looking for the highs but all the negatives of life come into play—and you don't *know* any negatives with the person, and that's why they cannot work, and they don't work. But because I had a child, I couldn't just leave, and I accepted that explanation fully from my counselor. If I had turned into my father? No way. Staying was a much better choice no matter what.

CHAPTER 18
From Sunnyside to Northridge

After Grandma and I got married, I desperately wanted to live in Bensonhurst, but there were no apartments. I just wanted to be in that neighborhood, but it was impossible. And then that apartment came up in Sunnyside, Queens. Grandma Rae had a friend who knew this lady who was moving out. The friend told Grandma that So-and-So was moving out because she bought a house, and Rae told us right away. She got the address for us, and we went down there immediately. That's how difficult it was to find housing at the time. It was either that or remain in the furnished room indefinitely, and that's when we decided to bribe the super with $700 cash to secure the apartment. It was only fifteen minutes from Manhattan. We were happy there. We were in better shape than the ones who ended up in Quonset huts, like the ones in Canarsie, Brooklyn. Even on Northern Boulevard, where I live now, they built them by the thousands, because there was no place for anyone to live anymore. The war was over, and people had no place to live from 1945 to 1950.

Everyone was having babies, but there was no place to live in New York city.

Compared to that, where we were living in Sunnyside was like the Taj Mahal: 15 minutes from Manhattan, three subway stops away. We had to move though, because it was only a one-bedroom apartment, and Grandma was pregnant again, with Teddy, so it was just too small.

The birth of my daughter Sharon in 1951 was the best thing that ever happened to me. I don't know about Grandma, because I can't get into her head. You know how good it was? The day she came home from the hospital, and I came home from work, and I walked into the apartment, and I saw the baby carriage in the living room—I remember it like it was yesterday—you know what crossed my mind? All the bad stuff that ever happened to me was no longer an issue. Everything was okay now. It took away every bad experience I ever had in my life, this one event. Everything is forgiven, because this was so powerful, just from looking at that baby carriage. I felt the slate is clean now, like I was starting all over again. The feeling didn't last, but I remember for a few moments, maybe even days, the slate was clean, and I was really on a high from having Sharon.

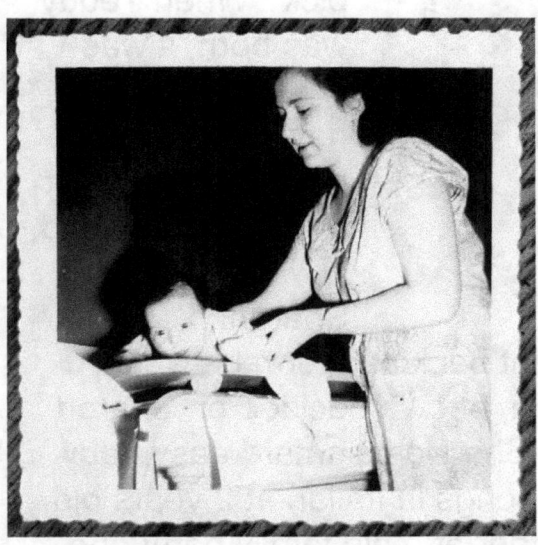

I remember Sharon as an infant crying in the middle of the night, and Grandma would say, "I'll walk with her in the foyer," but I'd walk with her in the foyer for about an hour. I couldn't get enough of her. In fact, when Grandma became pregnant with Teddy, my friends were saying, "Well, now you'll get a boy!"

And I said, "I want another Sharon! I don't want a boy."

Sharon was so great. She was so easy and she was smart; she was *everything*. Why wouldn't I want another one like that if I could have my pick? When Teddy was born, it was fine. It was *fine* to have a boy. But I never said, "I want another girl." I said, "I want another Sharon!" I remember we went back and forth between Sharon and Sheila, but we decided on Sharon. She was perfect. She was a smart, easy baby. She was singing songs in Italian at 2 years old. We were all together at a big family party one time, and she got up and sang *Eh, Cumpari!*, and everyone flipped out. Sharon was a genius.

How I Missed the War ... Again

I could have been drafted into the Korean War, but somehow I missed that too. The Korean War started in June 1950, and I had a 3A because they had had enough personnel in the military at the time, so they stopped the draft. But the 3A is right before the 1A, and I would have been drafted. But then Sharon was born, and it remained 3A. So maybe somehow they knew I was a new father, because I was never drafted. They did not take fathers.

The Koran War ended sometime around the middle of 1953, and Grandma got pregnant with Teddy sometime in 1954. So, I missed the opportunity to see Korea, but I understand from the guys who were there that it was a blessing I missed it. They called Korea "the Asshole of the World." It was a terrible place, at least at the time, not because of the war, just in general. The reputation of that place ... put it this way, they would never take a vacation there, even without the war.

Big difference from my missed opportunity after World War II. One friend stayed in a castle in Bavaria after the war, and another friend stayed in Hotel Manila, the largest luxury hotel in the Philippines. They were the conquerors, and every day was like a party for two straight years.

We Needed to Move

Grandma was pregnant with Teddy when we had to move out of Sunnyside, and that's when we found the apartment where I'm still living now. We moved here in 1954 and in September 2023 it's going to be 69 years that I'm living in this same apartment. Rae and Joe had already been living in this apartment complex in Northridge for the past two years. Rae knew we were looking to move, so one day she picked up the phone and told us there was an apartment available right across the street from her, and so we moved there. I wasn't thinking about the impact this would have on Grandma. I was only thinking about the perks of this new neighborhood for the kids.

The new apartment and the surrounding neighborhood had everything for Sharon and Teddy. I didn't know at the time what it would be like to actually live across the street from this monster—I mostly knew the things I was told about her. Grandma told me later on that we should have moved to California. All I could see was that there was a playground a block away, a sitting area right outside the window, a school a block away ... but for all the years we lived here or at least until Rae finally died, Grandma regretted having moved here. She went along with it because *I* wanted it. I thought it was going to be good for the kids, and once we were here it was too late.

Once we tried to move out, when both kids were under 10. I had friends in New Jersey, but we couldn't find what we wanted. But going fast forward to today, I'm *so* glad I'm here. It did work out for us in the end. Grandma Rae died in the early 1990s, and from the early 1990s until Grandma Rita died in August 2022, so for about 30 years, we really enjoyed this place immensely. So I'm more than glad that we did move here, because as a senior, all the help I get that is senior-related is just a phone call away. All I have to do is call NORC—Naturally Occurring Retirement Community. The goal of NORC is to keep people out of nursing homes so they can remain in their homes. That's the goal of this organization. And that's what they do.

CHAPTER 19
Our Life in Northridge

Grandma became pregnant while we were still living in Sunnyside. I remember we were so excited to move to Northridge, but looking back, I can see that Grandma was probably excited because *I* was excited. I wasn't able to think about the move from Grandma Rita's perspective. If I wanted something badly enough, I felt I could have it. But looking at the situation now, I realize, "She's going back to the devil that brought her up," while all I have in my mind are the perks: there's a school a block away, Sharon wasn't far away from being able to walk to school, there was a park right there, and we had our pick of apartments. Besides the school and playground a block away, our kitchen window looked right over the sitting area, so it was ideal for raising young children. There were only 2 apartments in the building that had an eat-in kitchen; the other 9 had dine-in foyers. So we were able to get the apartment with the eat-in kitchen, and we moved into the apartment in September 1954.

The reason we were able to get our pick of apartments was an unusual circumstance: a letter had circulated to everybody in the building that, due to some error and a shortage of funds, management was forced to institute an 18% rent increase. And so half the people moved out. When people came there in 1954, they came from where they were born, where they had been paying half the rent compared to Northridge. So most of the people who came to Northridge were already paying double what they were used to, and then they wanted to raise it another 18%. So Grandma Rae said to Rita, "Come and live here. Half the people moved out, and you can have your pick of apartments." Rita, passive person that she was, wasn't able to say no to her mother.

Teddy was born on January 6, 1955, just a few months after we moved in. Sharon and Teddy were three years and two months apart. It was a very hectic, hectic time. First of all, Grandma Rita had a more difficult pregnancy with Teddy. She didn't go through the nine months with no problems. She wasn't bed-ridden, but she had to be careful about something, and I didn't remember what it was. She ended up having

Teddy without any problems. But there was something off in the birth, and Teddy had to be checked frequently, with some kind of an illness. It wasn't serious, because I can't even remember what it was. But after Teddy was born, everything was okay for a while.

I was 25 and Grandma was 24 when we had two little ones. First, we were paying double the rent. I had a new car, a 1953 Hudson Jet, brand new in 1952 when I bought it for $2,200. I had this car in Sunnyside, and I had had it not even one year in Northridge. I had to take a second job just to make ends meet, and even with that I wasn't making ends meet, so I had to get rid of the car, because I wasn't able to afford it anymore, but I kept the second job. I was coming home 9, 10 at night, leaving the house at 6 in the morning, and I kept that second job until I had my mental breakdown.

Technically I blamed Grandma, a lot later on, for this terrible move, because I didn't understand why she didn't warn me about how horrible this woman Rae was. Instead she just passively let me have my way to move there, and I didn't know what I was getting us into. She grew up like this, and I felt like she could have warned me. Much later, she realized the mistake. She said, "We had a chance to move out of Sunnyside, and that was when we should have moved to California."

Grandma Rae was a very powerful control freak, and we were in our young twenties and didn't have the tools to resist her. She did this with us and with her own friends. But the thing was, one of the ways she attracted us was by saying, "I'm right across the street...I can babysit..." But we never went out. We had a built-in babysitter right across the street, but it ended very, very soon. She babysat, and we could see that she wasn't happy doing it. I can say she babysat for about a month. We should see it written all over her face that she didn't want to do it, so we just stopped asking her. She used this tactic as a ruse to get us there, not because she *wanted* us there, but because we represented more people she could control.

But fortunately for us, there were a lot of young families here, and what we ended up doing was trade babysitting with each other. And Rae never came back and asked why we never brought the kids over anymore. Whatever disappointments I had (like having to give up the car) didn't overshadow all of the perks that the apartment had to offer the kids. The damage was done in terms of Grandma and me, and it lasted for many years. I was able to handle the normal stuff, but she was *not* normal stuff. We really should have gone to California, like Grandma said. But I felt like a victim in the whole thing because the reality of living across the street was so much worse than I ever could have imagined.

Rae was a mental case—definitely. She had something against females, a strong dislike for females. And Grandma was so unwanted, even more unwanted than her younger brother Stuart.[4] Stuart said once, "The best mother I ever had was my sister—it wasn't my mother." He also told me that when Rita married me, he felt like I was his

---

[4] The picture is of Grandma Rita and her brother, Uncle Stuart.

father. The two of them were completely unwanted. The only one she ever wanted, the love of her life, was Theodore, the one who got killed in the war.

When I was dating Grandma Rita—she told me everything and never held anything back, because she had nobody—Rita told me that her father Joe told Rae: "We lost a diamond, and we got a piece of glass." I was the piece of glass. This was shortly after Theodore died, when it was still fresh. It was not a loving relationship. I shut the both of them out relatively quickly after we moved into Northridge in 1954, though they got a lot of chauffeuring around out of me, while I still had the car. They would talk, and I would tune them out.

Grandpa Joe was a weak man. There was a story that your mother Sharon told me recently. They went to the World's Fair, not the original one in 1939-1940, which I went to, but they all went to this new one around 1955-1956, and all of them went: Joe, Rae, Sharon, Teddy, a visiting cousin, and maybe Rita too, but I didn't go. So they were walking around at the fair, and at one point, Joe looked around and he could not see the El train, and he had a panic attack; he went into a full-blown panic attack.

Fast forward to the end of his life. The details of how he ended his life are simple. They were getting older now, and Rae was losing her victims one by one. They were all dying. He didn't want to give up his barber shop, because he didn't want to be near her. But she kept pushing and pushing for him to retire, and he kept resisting and resisting. But nobody could resist as much as she could push. It turned out to be a nightmare for that man. He would go the supermarket four or five times a day, every single day, just to get away from her. She drove him crazy. Just as an example, every time he opened his mouth, she'd say, "Shut up, Joe." Every time. I'll never forget it.

One day he finally snapped. Before he left the house to end his life, he picked up a table and threw it across the room at her. Then he walked out of the house and threw himself in front of a train. And as soon as she was told what had happened, the first words out of her mouth were, "Now what am I going to do?"

It's not an exaggeration to say that Rae killed her husband. She murdered him by driving him to suicide. You can say she was a witch because she *was* capable of driving people to suicide.

But we had our own lives as long as we kept the two of them out of it. Fortunately, we didn't live in the same building. But thanks to the last 30 years or so, it turned out to be the best of all possible moves, because we have NORC, and you can't have NORC if you don't live in the co-op. Once Rae died around 1992, everything was fine.

In the counseling world there's an illness called "Arrested Development," and I believe very strongly that Grandma was a victim of that, because I can't explain how she could have allowed us to move across the street from that woman, knowing what she knew about her. But she wasn't able to stand up against her or think for herself. She was completely under her thumb. She developed to a certain point and then never went any further. The only time she was ever happy was when I was happy. She was never happy with anything for herself. I was her whole life, 100%. So because I wanted to move to Northridge, this made her happy. And she wasn't able to realize what a nightmare this was going to be. It was a kind of magical thinking that if this made me happy, everything would be okay. But it was not okay.

Grandma did go into therapy many years later, when I was in therapy. She thought it was a success, and she got it into her mind that she solved all her problems. She did it for me, but it was a waste of time for her and a waste of time for the therapist. She was beyond help. She was so damaged from way, way back. She recognized that she needed help, and so she went based on a doctor's recommendation in the late 1960s or early 1970s. She went religiously for two straight years. But when it was over, she was exactly the same.

In much later years, two years before she went to the nursing home, the therapist who was seeing me agreed to see Rita, and this time she did it for me entirely, because she was convinced she didn't need it. And that was a total waste of time, too.

I mean, this issue that she had didn't affect my life. We had a great life, and for a while—about 10 years—we had great, great vacations together. We went to Florida for the whole month of May, we rented a furnished apartment close to the beach, only $1,000 for the whole month of May, paid in cash. And we did this for five years in a row every May. After that, we'd take 10-day vacations to Salt Lake City, Utah, where my family was. Three or four times a month we went to Yonkers Raceway. And about a dozen times we went to Las Vegas. I did all the planning. She didn't care where we went, so long as I was there with her. In the 1990s we had a lot good, good years. She made life very easy for me in the sense that anything I wanted, I could do. As long as I was happy, she was happy.

I had a very long period where I was out Thursday nights with my lodge, running a stock investment club with about 22 members, once a month, and every Friday night there was poker in somebody else's house, for 30 years—paddleball on Saturdays and Sundays, in the playground a block away, and she was fine. She stayed home, and she was fine with what I was doing the whole time. She just wanted to see me happy.

On the Jewish holidays, you're not supposed to play paddleball. You go to the synagogue. So on the Jewish holidays we all went to another neighborhood to play paddleball. They called us hypocrites; I would have been happy to stay right there in the neighborhood playing paddleball, but I was overruled. We went to Bayside, Forest Hills, and so forth, instead. Nobody knew us there.

Grandma never worried when I would be here, there, and everywhere, and I could go wherever I wanted. But after she had that stroke on May 12,

2010, and she was in that hospital for 66 straight days, in a couple of different hospitals actually, she changed. When we came home I thought the familiarity of her own place would work wonders for her, but it went the opposite way. She didn't know where anything was, not even the dishes. The stroke changed her, and she never got better. She had brain damage. And that's when she never let me out of her sight. I went from complete freedom to total captivity. I couldn't even go to the supermarket or do anything. I couldn't be out of her sight for a minute. It was a prison.

At one point I finally said to her, "I *have* to go, and *I'm going*." Teddy gave me his cell phone. I didn't deal with her. I told her, firmly, "I do all the shopping. Who's going to shop for food?" And she got quiet. I told her I'll ring the phone every half hour, and she was satisfied with that. I'd call her every half hour, and as soon as she heard my voice, she was calm.

That stroke finished her off, and had I not stood up to the imprisonment in the apartment, it would have finished me off, too. And I'm sure she was a nervous wreck in between phone calls, but I found a way out. She wasn't supposed to have survived the stroke. The doctors don't understand how she lived, because the stroke was so massive. But for five to ten years this went on, and I got used to it. I would go out, and I'd call her. We got into a routine, and it became normalized. But I have no idea what she was like between phone calls. I couldn't think about it, because I had to do what I had to do. If it had been paddleball, I would have given it up, but I had to do the basics: food shopping, doctor's appointments, and the like.

My Mental Breakdown

Getting back to life in Northridge, within five years of moving to Northridge we started to deeply regret it. This was right around the time of my breakdown, somewhere around 1959. Moving into Northridge caused me to double my normal living expenses, with no increase in my income, so I took a second job to help pay the bills here. But even though my rent was double, my income from the second job wasn't double. So I had to sell my car, and all of the stress I was under caused an anxiety situation. I went to the doctor to check me out, and he gave me this "miracle drug" called Thorazine, which was specifically meant to treat anxiety. But in my case, it doubled my anxiety. Shortly after taking the drug, I was driving, and I had a massive panic attack. I immediately stopped taking the Thorazine, but by then the damage was already done.

The next day after the panic attack, I found myself having mental problems. For example, I'd add a column of figures at work, and I kept getting the wrong answer, and then I'd do it a second time, and over and over, and I couldn't get the right or the same answer, so at a certain point I went into a depression. I was very, very frightened, and I knew I had to do something about this, because now I'm dealing with anxiety *and* depression.

My in-laws knew of a psychiatrist; I didn't even know what a psychiatrist was, but I went along. They took me to see him, and he wouldn't treat me. He was a high-priced doctor, and he wouldn't treat me because I didn't have the money. But he recommended someone who could help me, a young guy who was just starting out. So I went to see this Dr. Gerald

Giges on 96th Street, between Madison and 5th Avenue, right off of Central Park, and I started seeing him once a week. But to compound the problem, I'm now not able to work, and I didn't have the $10.00 for the visit. So I went to my brothers, and they would give me the money, but I promised to pay them back. I went to see this doctor for about six months, and at one point I asked him to hospitalize me. But he explained that he can't recommend hospitalization because what I have (emotional disturbance) is going to get better, and it did. It took another few months before I started coming out of it.

I gradually started working again, first a couple of hours a day, and then more. But then came a very bad decision on my part. As I was getting back to myself, I said to him, I don't think I'm going to come back. He warned me that this was a very bad idea. But I told him, I don't have the money for this, and I have to pay all this money back. If I feel well enough to get back to work, then I can straighten myself out financially. He warned me that if ever there was a good time to be doing this therapy, it's now, "because your head is clearing, and you're capable of really being in counseling and understanding everything. This is the worst time you could pick to leave."

But I left. I paid everybody back, and I "lived happily ever after." But he was right, because I did end up in therapy 20 years later and remained in it for many years, and I got worse. I mean I did well and everything else, but I could have done well 20 years earlier. I probably could have managed it because I was working again, but at the time I had had enough. But I recognize now that it was a mistake. I must have left him sometime in late 1959.

CHAPTER 20
The Societal Breakdown of the 1960s

The early 1960s—'60, '61, '62—were fairly uneventful for me. I had a job in Passaic, New Jersey, working a union job. Someone in that job approached me and gave me an opportunity, *non-union,* to go to work in my field (cutting in the garment industry) in Hoboken, New Jersey. It was a very lucrative setup, and I spent those early years working in someone else's place, but I was getting paid for every garment I cut. I was getting paid by the piece. And I started earning big, big money there.

I was working some long days. I was back to driving again, and I was leaving the house every day at 6 in morning and getting home to Jackson Heights at 10 at night. A normal salary at the time was $125 a week. I was making $800 to $900 a week in those few years. It was very tough, but I was making *so much* money. It was almost like I had my own business, but it was not my business, and so I didn't have to pay the rent on that space. I had a partner at the time, and we would split the money. It ended when they took a larger loft deeper into New Jersey, while at the same time they wanted to cut my pay, so I just couldn't do it anymore. I went back to my Manhattan cutting jobs right around 1964. The Passaic job I couldn't go back to. It was gone.

It bothered me a lot to lose that money. I got used to the big money. So I had misgivings about giving it up. It was an adjustment to get back to family life, but mostly I was stuck on all the money that I lost. There was nothing special going on at home in 1964. Personally speaking, the difficult times came a little later.

Difficult Times for the Country

When Kennedy was assassinated, it was a very dramatic time for the country. I remember the exact moment of being out to lunch in the garment center. I had just come back from lunch when I heard about the assassination, and I'll never forget my boss's comment when the news came over the radio: "I hope it wasn't a Jew who did it." That was his concern. That's because, if you're a Jew, it's a treacherous life that you live, even here in America. The mindset, at least for him, was that if a Jew did it, all of America would turn on the Jews, and I'll just never forget that comment.

The assassination happened on a Friday, and that was the night for the bowling league. I remember the mood. We went anyway, but it was a very, very, very rough weekend, as the news was registering with people and everything else—with people watching the news and stuff. It affected me like it affected everyone else. I remember my sister-in-law Terri, Sid's wife, had had a dinner planned for that Sunday night, and I was very, very unhappy going to that dinner, because my father was there along with my stepmother. That was one ugly weekend for me. The dinner happened on November 24, 1963. President Kennedy was killed on November 22.

By this point, society was already starting to fall apart. But there was no connection to the Kennedy Assassination in terms of triggering any kind of a downfall. The change downhill was already in motion. The young people were already going to Greenwich Village to hang out with the Beatnik Generation. Kids were flocking there from all neighborhoods. That's where all the action was. All the radicals were there, all the

Beatniks, and it escalated. It was the beginning of where we are now: the downfall started around when the 50s ended and the 60s began.

The Baby Boomers vs. Teddy

The post-World War II children were brought up differently. Teddy was different from the other kids, though. In 1961 and 1962, I had some kind of an arrangement to cut children's coats and snowsuits. I was almost partly in business with another guy on their premises. I got paid by the piece; I didn't have a salary. And I remember I was making piles of money. And for a time, I would take Teddy to the bowling alley every Friday. And I would give him money, and I asked him at one point, "How would you like to go to work with me tomorrow?" I was working in Hoboken at the time. He was under 10 years old, but he said he really wanted to go. And when we got there, I told him to take a broom, and asked the owner if he wanted the floor swept up, and the owner said, "Yeah, sure." So I told the owner to give him $2.00 when he was finished. Teddy was hooked for life when he got that $2.00. He was just like me, when I got my first dime. And after that he was up early every Saturday morning and went with me to work. He had a strong work ethic.

In 1967, Pizza Sam came to the neighborhood and opened up a shop on Northern Boulevard. Teddy got involved there, and as little as he was, he was now delivering pizzas at 12 years old. He would deliver anywhere he could walk. The point here is that this is the Baby Boomer generation, and a lot of the younger fathers came to me around 1967—by this point, I'm close to 40, and these were the fathers of some of the younger kids—and they would say to me, "How can you let him do that? He's only 12 years old. He has plenty of time to work!" I remember how they were all mortified. They used to watch me, and they were actually offended that I let him work. Teddy had all his friends, and he took part in the playground just like all the other kids, but he had this innate work ethic. I didn't drum it into him. And he was the only one among his peers who was like this.

Teddy never brought any of his friends into the house. But with Sharon, all the kids were there, and Rita was right in the middle of them. She'd sit in the living room with them. But they were nothing like the kids I grew up with. They were wild and screwy. Parents were reading these books like Dr. Spock and other books like this. This generation was raised by books, and the parents just followed whatever the books said. And this is what resulted: this generation.

Another "terrible" thing I did, which is how my friends would have put it if they had known about it, was this: when Teddy was 16, I told him, "You have to start contributing to the house: rent, food, and everything else." So he said, "If I have to contribute to the house, I may as well get my own place." So Grandma went to the closet and started taking out suitcases. When Teddy saw the suitcases, he relented and agreed to pay. And so I took money from him every single week. It was an arrangement. Age 16 represented full adulthood to me; to him, it was only partial adulthood.

In the second half of the 1960s, the house was full of kids, all Sharon's friends, all the time, and I didn't want to be near them. I thought they were all crazy. Willy,[5] Ellen, Robbie, Kathy, all of

---

[5] In January 1970, a little over two years after I was born, my mother Sharon married Willy. They had my half-sister Janina in 1973.

them, and Grandma was in the middle of all of it. I'd go in the bedroom and shut the door, and I just thought they were all crazy. "These 13-, 14-year-old kids," I thought, "They're off the wall, especially compared to the kids of my generation."

It was a bad time. It was not a pleasant time. Everything was going down the toilet, and it was affecting my daughter, not really my son. I remember when the majority of them decided to go to Colorado. Sharon didn't go, and Kathy didn't go, but most of them went. That was a major thing that happened.

Grandma was very, very much involved in all of this stuff that we're talking about, and I kind of dissociated myself. I didn't want to deal with it at all. Grandma really, really stepped up and became *the* important parent of the two of us. She stepped in and was involved and helped Sharon in any way she could. She knew that I didn't want to deal with it, so she never brought any of it up to me. She shielded me from what was going on, because she knew how I felt, so she left me out of it. I still don't know to this day everything that went on. I didn't accept the world that I was seeing, even though my own child was involved.

At first, the problem was just that they were all weird, but when Sharon was really in crisis, pregnant with you at 15, Grandma Rita completely stepped up and took over everything, which was *very* uncharacteristic of her. She was like the Rock of Gibraltar. Normally I had to lead and do everything. But I had to concentrate on my work; I didn't want to know, and almost didn't care, because I absolutely couldn't handle it. All my life, it was one chapter after another, and this was just too much. And I'm very grateful that it all ended well, but the in-between was tough. This went on the whole second half of the 1960s until the end of the decade, and then it all started to get better.

During those years I became very close to Teddy. He knew everything that was going on, and I got really close to him. The crisis going on in the family was the catalyst that caused me to really bond with him. He was with me every Friday night in the bowling alley. We had a Northridge league, and there were kids everywhere who went. I used to give him a couple of bucks for the game machines, and he had a ball.

The last night of this one particular bowling season, the first place team and the second place team were very, very close before the three games started. You bowled three games every week. When the third game ended, the other team claimed victory, and I asked to see the score sheet, because the last time I looked at that sheet that night, as the game was coming to an end, I saw that the exact scores that the two teams were at, and I can't remember 100% now, but it looked like we were winning this thing.

So I said, "We got this, we won this thing!" But then it ended, and the other team claimed victory. I said, "Wait a minute, we were up a certain amount of pins, and according to my arithmetic, you didn't win this thing." So I said to the captain of the other team, "Where is the scoring sheet that is always here?" And he said, "I don't know—in the excitement, it's gone." And I said, "Who would get rid of the sheet? It's always here!" So we went back and forth, and the sheet is nowhere to be found. How does an innocent sheet disappear? The prize money at the time was between $500 and $1,000 and that was in 1962, so it was a lot of money. I said, "This is absolute bullshit!" Anyway, they prevailed, I don't know how, and I don't know why; I don't remember. I said, "I'm through. I won't be back here next year. This is highway robbery—I don't understand a piece of paper disappearing when that piece of paper would have always been there, and it was there on all the other tables. I played in this league for five to six years." They said to me, "Why should we believe your arithmetic?" So I said, "You're right; I can't prove my arithmetic, and you can't prove you won." I said, "I won't be back here. This is a crooked operation."

So I went back to the apartment building, and the other guy, Artie Cohen, lived in apartment 204 (I live in 209), so we are on the same floor in the same building. I went back home and I went to sleep. At 2 in the morning, my bell rings. And Artie says to me, "Look, I don't want you to be upset." And I said, "I feel I was robbed. I did the arithmetic, and I feel like I was robbed because that sheet disappeared and it had no reason to disappear." And he said, "Look, we're all friends." And I said, "Artie, listen to me, I feel very strongly that we won this thing—by under 10 points—and we *did* win this thing." And I said, "I'm not coming back," and I had bowled with these people for 10 years.

I used to be a bowling junkie. I kept a bowling ball in the trunk of my car. But that night finished me. I never wanted to go back after that. That's what ended my bowling career. I stayed neighborly with him, but it was never the same. We were never friendly after that. There were five guys on the other team who ripped us off, and if I had to pick out which one of them was the one who did the cheating, I would have picked Artie. I think he was behind it.

Out With Bowling, In With Paddleball

I stumbled down to the playground after that, and I used to watch the paddleball players. I took it up, but I couldn't become a paddleball player with the men—they were all too good. So what I did was when daylight savings time came, I'd come home around 4:30, I'd change my clothes, and I'd tell Grandma that I'd have supper when I came back. The girls loaned me a paddle, and I started playing with these 14- to 15-years old girls. There were four girls on the court, and there would have been another six waiting to play. My partner, Sharon Liss, is now 70, so I was 25 years older than all of them. All of these kids were from Northridge. I didn't know any of them, but they knew me—they knew me as Sharon and Teddy's father.

I played with them for a couple of months, and I became better and better. After about three or four months, I moved over to play with the men. I was good enough to be with the male group. So it was like I had gone to paddleball school for three or four months. The girls gave me the basis that I needed, five afternoons a week. I couldn't practice with them on Saturdays and Sundays because the men had all four courts.

So that's how I switched sports. I played paddleball for 20 years. I had to quit at age 60 because of a pinched nerve in my neck. The guys I played with all those 20 years went on to play into their 70s. Even after I stopped, I still went down there to watch them for a little while but then I eventually stopped. It was too frustrating to watch them and not be able to play.

A Love of Walking

That's when Grandma and I started our walking career. That walking we did for *years*. These walks were very long. We always stopped to share a blueberry muffin and coffee wherever we went. Every Saturday and Sunday, the Museum of the Moving Image in Astoria showed old movies from the 1930s and 1940s, and we went every Saturday and every Sunday, and I would say that's about five miles from home, so five miles there and five miles back every Saturday and Sunday when we were between 60 and 70 years old. When I retired in my late 60s, we walked distances even longer than that. We even walked to Queens Boulevard; we would walk up and down Queens Boulevard, and we would be gone for hours. Another time we went to see Emeril Lagasse in the West Village up 6th Avenue, and so on, about 80 blocks, and we did this kind of walking routinely.

In the early 1990s, after Grandma Rae died, I rented an apartment in Fort Lauderdale, completely furnished, and we would walk for I have no idea how long, but we would walk for three hours, and then we would go from town to town and then walk back. We never took buses; we walked everywhere. These walks definitely affected my open heart surgery on the positive side. I remember the surgeon said that the surgery was going to be a piece of cake for me, and it was. I had triple bypass surgery at age 78, and I was out of the hospital in four days.

I remember you calling me on the day of the surgery. I was scheduled to be number 3 and I remember you called me about 1 in the afternoon, and I took the phone in the hospital, and just before you called, the doctor came over to me—and I was not too happy being number 3 and being the last patient being operated on that day—and I remember this so clearly, he came over to me and he said, "I just want to let you know that we moved you up to number 2," and then right afterwards you called. Then I said to you, "This is some kind of lucky charm call, you calling me, because these two things were five minutes apart." I couldn't have been happier that my surgery was moved up. I said to you, "You're my lucky charm!" I remember that so clearly. That was in 2006. I must have had the surgery on a Thursday, and you came up to see me in the hospital on the weekend after the surgery.

Grandma and I walked after dinner every night on top of the monster walks we did on the weekends and in Florida. These walks were easy and normal for us. They had to have some long-term benefits for both of us, as it would be the case for everyone who does that.

Grandma's First Real Job

Grandma got her first real job in the 1960s. She worked on 57th Street between Madison and 5th Avenue. The company was Genesco, a huge international apparel company with 18,000 employees worldwide. She did not go out to look for a job. I don't think she would have gone to work if it were up to her, but there was a neighbor across the street who knew her well, and she got the job for her. Grandma's number one thing was her low self-esteem, and her number two thing was her passivity. It was a very good thing that this job came along, because I don't think she would have gotten a job on her own. She worked there for 10 years in Credit and Collections. She did fabulously, even though she told her boss when she was offered the higher position, "I can't do it." The boss said to her,

"You can do it, and you're *gonna* do it." So she accepted the promotion.

But that low self-esteem that was drilled into her since she was a little girl never went away. I mean, I had a background too, but I sure had my self-esteem. We were totally opposites. I was more like a parent to her than a husband. It wasn't good. I once said to her, "It's really amazing how well you're doing on that job. I said you should really give yourself a pat on the back. You deserve it." Silence.

So I said, "You know what? Take the palm of your hand and just do it, pat yourself." And she wouldn't answer me, and she wouldn't do it. She *couldn't* do it. So I got up, and I patted her back. I said, "If you can't pat yourself on the back for that great job you're doing, then I have to pat you on the back." But it was amazing. I was stunned. No expression. She was just staring into space. I'll never forget it. She had a lot of problems. Tremendous, tremendous damage was done to her that could not be undone.

Grandma would never have left Genesco. She would have worked there until she could retire. She loved that job; she loved going to work in the morning. It did something for her, being in that high position.

The only reason she stopped working there was that the company was in financial trouble. The founder of the company handed the operation over to his son, and his son turned out to be a Hollywood playboy. And literally within two to three years the son wrecked that business. The stock went from $70 to $80 a share to $3 a share in less than three years, so they closed her division. The company eventually bounced back, but by then it was too late for her to go back to her old job.

Grandma's Friend Julie

Grandma met Julie at Genesco. They worked together in the Credit and Collections department, where Julie was Grandma's boss. Julie was brought over to the Manhattan branch from the Philadelphia branch, because the married boss, who lived in New York, was having a fling with Julie in Philadelphia. So he had her moved to the Manhattan branch so it would be easier for him to keep seeing her. It turns out Julie didn't know anything about the job. Whenever anyone had a question, Julie would say, "Go ask Rita," and Rita would always have the answer. Eventually the same boss transferred Julie to another department, so Grandma took over Julie's job, despite her lack of confidence. Thankfully, the boss didn't take "I can't" for an answer. That's how Grandma took over the entire department.

After her promotion, when her father Joe found out how much money Grandma was making, he said to her, "*You? You're* making all this money?" It wasn't exactly parental approval. It was more like he was saying, "*You?* The family *imbecile?*" That was the praise she got from him.

The fact that Grandma took over Julie's job had no bearing on their close friendship. They remained close friends from the late 60s to the late 70s—all the years while Grandma was working at Genesco—and then all the way through until Julie died, which was about ten years ago. Julie and her husband Arthur used to come up to the apartment all the time and we'd go out to dinner with them near their place, or we'd have dinner at home here. We all had a great time together.

In terms of why this particular friendship was so strong and lasted so long, all I can say is that Julie was the opposite of Grandma; she was very outgoing, and Grandma was attracted to her personality. Their friendship had nothing to do with me at all. It was their close friendship, and that's how I became close friends with her too, and then with Arthur, when the two of them got married. We liked being together, and we'd get together regularly.

Julie knew all about Grandma's troubled past, and she hated Grandma Rae. She hated all of them—the whole family did a number on Grandma, including the aunts and uncles (Rae's brothers and sisters). They all treated her like the family idiot.

Two Kinds of Abuse

Grandma and I never fought. *She* fought. I didn't fight. I never went one-on-one with her. She would just explode. She had a short fuse. All her life, when we were married, she would just explode. You'd get used to it. It wasn't often, but it was frequent enough that you'd remember. It got a lot better as she got older, especially with our vacationing. Even though we were both abused as children, she was explosive, and I was not. My abuse was total neglect. And this neglect didn't bring about an explosive trauma response, like it did in Grandma.

Grandma expressed her first feelings when she met me. Over the previous 15 years of her life, she was shut down. She went silent; she would not talk. She was so silent that at one point someone said to her, "I didn't know you could talk!" So her damage was so tremendous, so much more than mine, that she shut down, and by the time she was an adult, the slightest, most insignificant things could result in an explosion, because she had all that pent-up anger. I had rage and she had rage, but my rage was directed at my parents and partially to my brothers, and to my stepmother—all parental—the so-called rage wasn't generalized. Once I was away from those blood and family relations, I did fine with people. People liked me, I liked them—the people in the candy store, the tailor, the pharmacy people, they liked me. I had a great, great, great "family" but no blood relatives. They liked me and they adopted me. The candy store was my second home.

Grandma, different from me, had trouble relating to everyone. Growing up, she was sexually molested all the time. And she was silent and lived with it. She always walked around different—she had trouble relating to people. One lady who lived on our floor told me about this one time when Grandma was standing in the hallway alone, and the lady was standing there with a baby carriage, and she was struggling, and Grandma was just standing there and wouldn't offer to help. Grandma had a kind of shyness that was beyond normal. She was looked on as a weirdo—and she was. I didn't see her that way, but in retrospect, looking back...she was.

Grandma was a loner. She was very comfortable being alone. All her mixing as an adult was with my friends. We had a houseful all the time. A lot of company. She cooked dinner for them, but they were all my friends. Every one of them was my friend. She never had one person in her life outside of me who was her friend until she met Julie on the job. That means she went all the way into the 1970s without a single friend except for Julie. I married her in 1949, and she had had some neighborhood girlfriends, but once we got married, all those girls disappeared. All her adult life, that houseful of people were all my friends—from the job, from the lodge—because I'm social. I'm really, really social. They became "our friends." I'm thinking Julie is the only true friend she ever really had. Julie was a lot younger than Grandma, but that age difference was meaningless to Grandma.

I don't know what Grandma would have done if she had never met me. She used to say that if she had never met me, she would have been like one of those "babbling idiots on the park bench." I didn't know what to say to her. But I think she would have been capable of suicide. She did go to counseling for two years, but she got nothing from it in those two years, even though she said she thought it helped.

But in totality I had a good life with her, especially in the later years, in the 1970s and 1980s, when it was just the two of us. I planned everything, and we went everywhere. She could have stayed home and done crossword puzzles all day long, but since I wanted to go everywhere, she wanted to be where I was—and she was only happy if I was happy.

A Double Birthday

When you were born, in 1967, I was around 180 pounds by this point. What stands out in my mind is that I was diagnosed with diabetes on September 22, 1967, and on the same day you were born. By January 1, 1968, a little over three months later, I had taken off 40 pounds. And I was really proud of myself. I remember walking past a storefront and not recognizing myself. It's important to mention the "birth" of diabetes on this day, because if I had never been diagnosed with it, I would have been dead a long time ago. Diabetes saved my life.

But the rest of the stuff from this decade is difficult to talk about, because there was a lot of legal stuff that was going on having to do with the crisis that was going in the family, and here I am working all the way in New Jersey, and I'm dealing with a difficult work situation, and I'm also dealing with a major family problem at the same time. I was basically overwhelmed. We had to talk to social workers. The subject is very heavy for me, so I can't really talk about it much, but after this period, after a short time, everything was normal again, especially as this decade came to a close.

I'd pick you up by around 3 or 4 every Friday afternoon. I remember you were very, very little; it was before your sister Janina was born. We had you alone in the house for sleepovers way, way before Janina was born. If Grandma was alive and lucid, she'd be able to answer a lot of this subject matter, because she was in it from day one. She was *so* out of character when she was like this. It just shows you what she was really capable of, and she didn't know it. Just like she was capable of taking that giant job, and really succeeding. She was exceedingly good at it.

 That was the tragedy of Grandma: what she would have been capable of. She would rise to the occasion, and when the occasion was over, she'd fall back into herself and become the person who can't do anything—unsure, insecure. Tragedy, such a real tragedy. Ninety years of insecurity. Horrible, horrible.

To sum up, the decade that I started off saying was not too eventful for me *did* turn out to be a lot, now that I think about it. But we got through it. I wasn't there emotionally through the whole thing. I was there *physically*. We went to the home where your mother Sharon was when she was pregnant with you. We went a couple of times. I think we were able to take her out for dinner. I have a memory that we could do that. I was there for all that stuff, but I wasn't "into" the whole thing like Grandma, but then again I was out there working and making a living, so how much strength was I expected to have? Grandma was a housewife at the time, so she was able to step in and step up. I was more like the chauffer. But the real getting into it was Grandma Rita, 100%. I was happy, and I was really proud of her.

Everything she was brought up with, she did the opposite with Mommy and Teddy. She did the total *opposite* in every way. I'm not saying that this necessarily worked well, but she consciously wanted to do completely the opposite of how she was raised. There's no perfection in this, but I think she was a great mother.

Sharon told me once that her only childhood memory of me is me in the dark: leaving the house in the dark and coming home in the dark. Every day except for Sundays. On Sundays, we had a whole game plan and we did a lot of things together. This went on for a couple of years: I worked 14 to 16 hours a day, and this was normal for me. There are a lot of gaps in what I can remember about these years ... because I wasn't there. Rita really is the one who brought them up. I can't even say I was a weekend father: I was a Sunday father.

Sunday Family Time

On Sundays it was the whole family together starting early in the morning. There was a very popular magazine at the time, called *Cue*, and they had all the things that were going on in New York. I'd get the magazine on Wednesdays, and I'd spend the next several days picking out where we were going to go and what we were going to eat. We used to go to Broadway shows in one of the hangers at Kennedy Airport, for example. We'd go to upstate New York. We went out to Long Island to an animal farm one time. I never had to wonder what we were going to do on Sundays. This went on up until around the end of 1966. We were a close-knit family, the four of us, when I was home.

The Vietnam War

The Vietnam War years were a very unhappy time, with a lot of teenagers going to Canada instead of serving. The Veterans who came home were spat upon by the American people. Soldiers—*our soldiers*—they were spat upon. That's how unpopular this thing was. It was a very bad time, an unhappy time.

I'll give you an example of what it was like. It was like it is now, and I'm talking about the temperament of the general population. Julie's friend Sue recently told me that her brother went to France during this time and never came back, just so that he wouldn't be drafted. It was just the opposite of World War II. The kids, all of them, were jumping at the chance to serve and be in there. This was the exact turn-around. Recently, not very recently, they got forgiveness from the government for being conscientious objectors of the war. I think it was under Clinton, because I think Clinton tried to leave for Europe, too.

The news was always watered down during these years. We never really knew what was going on. The media during that time ... the media was the same bullshit like it is today. Because when you go back into the real history of the Vietnam War, it was so much more horrible than how they were making it sound on the news. And the tragedy was that we never should have been there in the first place, or caught up in it at all.

When the Vietnam war was going on, though, I was approaching middle age and I didn't have children going into the service, so it was relatively minor compared to the other things that were going on during those years in terms of their importance in my life.

CHAPTER 21
My Business Ventures

The 1970s were quite possibly the most interesting years of my life. Let's start off with 1971, where I'm home on my usual industry layoffs. The garment industry usually had layoffs between seasons; we'd get laid off and collect unemployment. One day—it was a Friday—I'm sitting on the couch, and I'm reading the stock pages in the *New York Times*, and at about 11:30 in the morning, about half an hour before lunch, before I put the paper away, I did something that I rarely do: I go to the want ads. I don't know why.

So I'm going through the want ads at random, and I come across an ad that said, "New York rep wanted for men's leather garment company." And I said to myself—because all my working life I'm making a living, but I don't like what I'm doing, always fantasizing about doing something else—"I'm gonna call up, just for the hell of it." And I make the phone call, and I get a gun-holster company on the phone, a manufacturing company based in Frederick, Maryland. I explained that I'm from the garment clothing industry, but I then said, "Apparently this phone call is meaningless, because you don't handle clothing."

But the man on the other line said, "Now, hold on, because you have reached the Buchheimer Gun Holster company. I'm the president, and it is garment-related in the sense that it was taken over by Tandy Leather, and we were asked to form a men's leather clothing company." He went on to tell me about the formation of this new company, now that Tandy owns them, a leather men's coat company from scratch. He told me they have an office right in the Empire State Building, and that they're looking for a New York sales rep to do this work. And I said, "I have extensive experience, all on the ladies side, none on the men's side. But that doesn't mean I can't go out to a buyers' office; it's just a different sales area, but sales is sales. But based on what you're saying, I think I can do this."

He asked me where I am located, and I said I'm in New York and very close to La Guardia airport. He said I seem interested, and he's interested, so he said, "How do you feel about possibly coming down here?" Meanwhile I was home for two weeks on unemployment. So I said, "When?" and he said, "How about today?" He went on, saying, "You live close to the airport. The flight from La Guardia to Dulles is one hour. You could be in Washington, D.C., in an hour, and I'm one hour away from Dulles Airport. I'll have one of my workers with a sign around his neck, and you'll just look for that sign." So I said, "Okay, I'm gonna do it."

The next part of the story is on the comedy side. Grandma's making lunch, and I come into the kitchen, and I say, "I'm not eating lunch; I'm going down to Frederick, Maryland." So she's flipping out and saying, "I don't believe this!" and I said, "I'll be home for dinner!" She's just standing there in the kitchen, not comprehending, but I explained the whole thing to her, and I went.

I spent a couple of hours with this guy, and he hired me. I'm at a point in my life where I really hate what I'm doing, and I'm hating it more and more, and I'm 42 years old. I said to myself, "I have to try this thing, and whatever happens, happens. I have to do this." I'm very unhappy with what I'm doing, so I accepted. He gave me the keys for the office in New York, and he said, "You'll be working in an office with a man about your age. He will be the designer, and you'll be in charge of sales. And the two of you are going to be running this office, Room 4524, in the Empire State Building." I was on a salary, and I started within days. I had to go up to the cutting union and I tell them I'm taking a leave of absence. They wanted the details, but I told them I couldn't give them any details. "I'm going into a business venture, and if it don't work out I'm coming back, back into the union like I did all these years." I cleared that up right away. Two or three days later, I'm in the Empire State Building trying to make contacts.

So we have eight salesmen on the road including me, and I'm the New York rep. I start going around to the buyers' offices—I know where these places are, and I know what to do—but I started to see in a relatively short time, after about a month, that this thing is *not* going to work. It's not going to work, because the whole Maryland-based operation was very unprofessional, not up to New York standards. So although I'm getting a salary, I'm not confident about my future.

So this guy I'm working with and I decided that we'd better talk to this guy, the president. He's born and bred in Maryland and he's a gun-holster guy. He doesn't understand how things work in New York. So we called him up, and we told him we want to have a face-to-face conversation, not on the phone. He asked if anything is wrong, but we said, "We want to come down and talk to you, and you have to agree to it without any further details." So he set up a meeting, and we went down there, and for some reason we met in a hotel room. And we told him how we feel, and he became very defensive and said, "You're not even giving this thing a chance!" But we said, "When we joined you, you already had seven salesmen on the road. And they never sold anything."

Dick Buchman was not only the president; he was also the sale manager. Everyone was getting $200 a week and 4% sales commission, but nobody was selling anything, so nobody was getting a commission. So we said to him, "What's to prevent the guys on the road from taking the $200 a week and not bothering trying to sell anything?" He said, "Well, that's unethical!" But he was so naïve. We knew that what this would lead to was that this parent company, Tandy, would just close the subsidiary. It would take them five minutes to make that decision.

Buchman got really defensive. He said, "Do you think you could do a better job than me as a sales manager?" So I said, "Blindfolded and with one arm tied behind my back," because I knew I was going to get fired anyway. "What would you do differently?" he said. And I said, "Number one, get rid of the cash and double the commission." So it ended up where he gave me the job, and I became the Sales Manager! And I called all these guys and told them the news: the $200 a week is gone, but we're doubling your commission. They all quit except for two guys, which was expected. So I said, "Okay, send your samples back to the company, and that's it, you won't be working for the company anymore."

I spent the next six months building up a new sales staff according to the new terms. And the way I was doing it, what was so wonderful about this, was I had to fly to all of these different cities to meet different people. They had to have some kind of experience, possibly in sales; I had criteria, and they had to sound interesting enough, and so I'd go to them. If they flew to me, they could bullshit me. Instead, they had to take me to the shops and stores they would be selling merchandise to.

So for a number of weeks, I'd leave, and besides my salary ($300 a week), I had an unlimited expense account, which I did not abuse, but it covered *everything*, and this thing was fantastic. So what I would do for the next couple of months? I'd leave La Guardia airport every Sunday night, and I'd go to a different city and stay there until Thursday. I'd spend three and a half days with these guys, and they'd take me around to all of the stores they would be selling to. I went to Minneapolis, Los Angeles, St. Louis, Atlanta, Dallas, Boston, a town in Maryland ... there were eight total places and I took about sixteen trips before Tandy came along and shut the whole thing down. They shut the whole thing down overnight while I was trying to build it up. And that was the end of that.

I had to go back to my cutting union, and I had to tell them, "It didn't work out, and I'm back." But without question, this had been the best six to eight months of my entire career. The comparison is easy to imagine: flying around the country staying in really nice hotels or being locked up all day in a factory.

I'll never forget St. Louis, Missouri. They had a dinner show in the hotel around mid-week, and I went in there for dinner. This female singer came out, and she was the star of the show, a variety show—and I know everything about music from my era—and she just *blew* me away. She was awesome. I went to the dinner show all three nights I was there, just so I could see her. I'll never forget her voice. On the last night I was there, I went to talk to her, and I said, "I know my singers, and you are sensational!"

I asked her if there was any possibility she would ever come to New York for any reason, but she told me there would be no reason she would come to New York by choice, because she has a family here. She told me she has all the work she could ever want in the Midwest, and that she is very happy with the setup here—no ambitions to make it big. So I said, "I just wish my wife could see you and hear you, because we are musical people, and you are the best singer I've ever heard." The big number she finished with was *Jesus Christ Superstar*. I'll never forget her—she was the most talented, best singer I have ever heard.

So these are the experiences I had. I saw the United States, which was great. If I had to do it over again, I'd do it in a heartbeat. In fact, I got a phone call when my situation ended—and I don't know who it came from, because I didn't investigate—from someone in the Tandy company. I didn't know they knew my name. So this Tandy person asked me if I'd be willing to relocate to Ada, Oklahoma. It was out of the question with that phone call. But this was the most memorable period of my life: 1971 to 1972.

I went back to my cutting job when it was all over, as I mentioned. By around 1975, I was getting very antsy in what I'm doing. Something's bothering me. I'm saying to myself, "I never really thought of going into business for myself. I'm tired of the rat race and the layoffs, but I also don't have any money to do anything."

Grandma Rae had a friend named Minnie. I used to drive this friend home to Brighton Beach from

Northridge. On one of these drives, Minnie asked me what I'm doing with my life, and I told her that I wanted to open my own cutting business instead of working for someone else. So she said, "What do you intend to do?" I told her that I don't have enough money, and that's when she asked me how much I needed. I said I'd need about $10,000 to start, because it would be a service business, without much overhead. I knew Minnie had money, but I never thought of her at all when I was going through this uneasy period. She offered me the $10,000, but she said she didn't want anyone to know about it. I refused the money, though. I was worried that I couldn't pay her back if the whole thing failed, but my antsiness became worse and worse. I ended up putting together a situation where I was *going to* rent space that had a cutting table and a couple of cutting machines. That's all I would need to get started. I didn't have any customers, but I started to go around in the trade to drum up work.

The Garment Center of Manhattan is all of five or six blocks. It goes from about 34th Street to 40th Street and then from 5th Avenue to 10th Avenue. It's small. I was going around to manufacturers, and I was approaching them and telling them I'm cutting for the trade, and if you need anything cut—your dresses, your sportswear—I have a cutting service. So they said, "Where are you located? And I said, "I don't have a place yet," so they weren't interested, because I didn't have a space.

But I did end up doing as I had planned. I rented a cutting table in a factory that belonged to these two old cutting guys: $300 a month in exchange for use of the cutting table and the telephone. And I *did* it. I put my name on the door, and I was in business. But I still had no customers, and I'm still paying this rent. So I went into the want ads for *Women's Wear Daily*, the trade paper, and I would read the ads every day. There were ads in the paper every day—manufacturers looking for sewing people and sewing factories to sew sportswear. Out of desperation, I started answering the ads looking for sewing people. In one case, I called up and said to the guy, I said, "I'm a contractor, and I'm local, but I'm not a sewing contractor," at which point he asked me why I'm wasting his time. "If I wanted a cutting contractor I would have put an ad in the paper for a cutting contractor," he continued.

But instead of getting discouraged by his reaction, I gave him a proposal. I said, "Suppose you had an overload of work, and you needed someone to help you cut. Where would you find them? Wouldn't you be glad that someone like me was there?" So he just said, "This is a ridiculous phone call." I said, "We can end the call, but take my number—you have nothing to lose."

He took my phone number, and two weeks later I got a call from him! He said to me, "Remember that conversation we had? I need a certain amount of samples cut, and I need it as quickly as possible. Do me a favor and have this done by tomorrow, and call me when it's ready." And that contact turned into why my business was successful for the next five years—that one contact that I made.

Shortly thereafter he called me again with an order for 100 t-shirts—these were all *right-away* orders—so I said to him, "I appreciate that you're giving me work, but I have customers now, and

I'm doing orders for some other people, but I'm going to do yours right away, because we have a relationship. (I didn't have any other customers—I was lying.) That became the beginning of a long relationship. His company's name was Lady Madonna, a big company. They had a specialty store on Madison Avenue run by a family, and from that one store they expanded to a giant, giant company to the point where they had stores overseas. My company became Artel Trimming. I only worked for Lady Madonna; that's how big they grew. They grew really, really big and were even selling franchises. They felt that if a woman is pregnant, that doesn't mean she shouldn't be fashionable—and nobody ever heard of that concept before. They became a giant, because nobody was doing this. They did jeans, and they were the first to create the net for the expanding bellies. The t-shirts were very big too.

As they grew, I grew. So now this little cutting table is not enough for me any longer. I was working 12 to 15 hours a day in the beginning, and I remember I was working on 38th Street and 8th Avenue, and Grandma's job was on 57th Street. She'd come up to my factory and help me because I couldn't afford to pay anyone, and she'd work for two to three hours after work. It was very, very tough in the beginning. I didn't draw any salary for about fifteen months.

Threatened by a Union Goon

One day this union guy came along and wanted to know what I'm doing there. I remember going back and forth with the guy, and at one point he threatened me physically, because these people are what they call "Union Goons"; they go around threatening people. And I said to him, "Why do you have to talk like a tough guy?" So he calmed down, and I said, "Tomorrow morning, let's go eat for breakfast, and we'll talk this over." And he got quiet, because he knew it was going to be a bribe. When he came in at 7 in the morning for breakfast, I gave him a handshake and slipped $100 in his palm. So he said, "You know what? You're a really nice guy, so I'm gonna try to help you, and I'll help you with advice." He said, "If you stay away and stay under 34th Street, nobody will go near you, and if you go above 40th Street, nobody will go near you," he said. "Nobody will bother you if you stay out of the guidelines where you can work without any trouble."

I thanked him very much, and that's when I found out about this place that became available, and it was only half a block away. I took over the whole place. It was only $2,000 to buy all the equipment and take over the lease. They had three 40-yard-long cutting tables and between seven and eight hand-cutting machines. I needed the expanded space and equipment because of this maternity account. They were feeding me enough work to need that size, and by this point I had five to six people working for me. But now I have the problem of having this nice big business right in the middle of a union area. So what do I do? I go to the super, and I say to him, "I don't want my name on my door, on the directory downstairs, *nowhere*." I gave him 25 bucks, and I spent the next five years with a nameless business—and I never got caught and never had any trouble. I had five to six fantastic years there, and all the while, nobody knew I was there. I gave the mailman 25 bucks too, and I told the mailman to give all my mail to the super, and I got away with it.

There is a tragic end to this story. In around late 1978, the owner of the company comes up to where I was working, and he says, "You're with us for a couple of years now, and we're getting bigger and bigger. We've gone international—Venezuela, advertising on TV, etcetera. We are very, very happy with your work, and we want you to take a bigger place." I said I'd have to think about it, and I also said, "If I say I don't want to do it, how will that affect our relationship?" "Not at all," he said, "but we just want to give you the opportunity to grow with us."

I told him no. I said one of the reasons is the cost. "I can't expand this place, and then I have to put all this equipment into it, and that's a small fortune." He said he'd pay for it, but I told him I didn't know how I'd pay him back. So he said he would take a percentage off of the invoices until I paid it back, and that seemed fair. But I remember talking it over with Teddy, and my gut feeling was not to do this. I said to myself, "Don't touch a good thing that's not going to go bad if I say no."

But right at that same time it ended up with a tragedy. Just before I was ready to meet with him to tell him I decided not to do this, the owner died of an overdose. He was only 38 years old. And that was pretty much the end of everything. The business went on without him, but it was not the same. Everything started to go downhill with his company, and that affected me. My lease was up in 1980, so I packed the whole thing in, and I started something new after taking all of 1981 off. I just took the whole year off.

New York City Streets in the Late 1970s

Before I get into the 1980s, I want to make a detour and talk about what New York City was like in the mid-1970s, from 1975 through the end of that decade, or at least what it was like for me.

I had two personal incidents not directed against me personally but against my business. For instance, I sent my worker a block away to a manufacturer to get 25 bolts of material for me to cut, and as he came back into my building, and as he went into the freight entrance, someone pulled a knife on him and took all 25 bolts, each having about 80 yards, and that was money that the manufacturer lost: a couple of thousand dollars. Another incident was, I came in one

Monday morning, and all my cutting machines were gone, about eight of them, and I had to replace them. I had a hint as to who it was and how it happened. I believe someone came down from the floor above me, because my floor had a balcony, so my theory is they came out of the floor above my balcony and got into my factory that way, and stole those machines.

Then there were the late nights when I was the last one in the building, sometimes at 9, 9:30 at night, and I'd take the self-service elevator down, and I'd close the building. The street would be deserted; I never had an incident, fortunately, but I easily could have. And also, someone set a fire, to a rubbish can, in my building on the third floor. They just tossed a match into it, and it was really scary. The fire department came. It was a terrible, terrible decade.

It was very similar to how it is now. When Giuliani became the mayor, he cleaned everything up. But the people who ran New York City were responsible for what happened to New York in the 1970s. The people finally elected a Republican to clean it all up. The frequency of the crime then is like it is now, but it's much more *vicious* now, with people getting pushed onto the train tracks and beaten. They are attributing what's happening now to widespread mental illness brought on by locking people up during the COVID pandemic. It's a mental health crisis, and they are saying that's why it's so bad now. During the COVID lockdowns, people were being jailed in their own houses. We're seeing the aftermath of that now in the horrific crimes that are all over the news. Even though the crimes are similar to what was happening in the 1970s, with people being pushed in front of trains and whatnot, I think the reasons are different.

CHAPTER 22
Easing Out of Work and Back Into Therapy

In 1980 they wanted me to sign a five-year lease in this same building, but I didn't want to do this for another five years, so I sold everything and took a whole year off and hung out with Grandma.

In 1982 I opened up a new business in Flushing, close to where I lived. The name of the business was Jan-Li Trimming. Grandma and I had Teddy working with us; I got in there in February 1982, which happened to be the beginning of a very horrible recession that we had in this country; I didn't have a clue what would follow. I started off the first month, and I was doing really good, with three or four customers, when all of a sudden, the people I was working for closed up. They were in Manhattan. And they closed up because that severe recession came on like a hurricane. It only lasted a couple of months, but it was bad enough for me to close up too. I then just went back to normal 9-to-5 jobs working for the union and finished up my working years over the next 10 years. I worked on and off, and by the end I was working a three-day week until I finally retired.

These last 10 working years were very good years as a semi-retiree. Grandma and I started vacationing to places we had never been to. During those years I rented an apartment, and we went to Utah and Fort Lauderdale regularly. It was a really memorable period for both of us. I had made a deal with the owner of the apartment, and I'd go off-season for a month, in May, and I paid cash. So I gave him $1,000, and I'd get there every May 1, and I'd give him $500 on May 1 and $500 on May 30. Every day we walked to the beach. It was great. And Utah was ten days every October, and we'd stay in a hotel. Salt Lake City is similar to New York. Even if the family wanted us to stay with them, we didn't want to. We wanted to be downtown.

I finally retired fully in 1993, when the people I was working for in the 1990s went out of business. Work-wise, it was over. I loved being retired. It was very easy for me. The flip side of it was that now that I wasn't working anymore, I started to have these emotional problems resurfacing. There's no way I could really explain what was happening, but starting in these years I went to counseling on my own, through an agency. They said they were going to have to give me a two-day evaluation to see what my situation was and who they would place me with—which therapist. The one "must" was definitely that it *had* to be a female. That was for sure. That's what they said after the evaluation was over. They didn't go into why, but it seems obvious that it was because of my issues with my father. And I spent the next 10 years or so in therapy until it ended in 2003.

The therapy was tremendously successful, and that's because I had the right person. I was with her for seven years, through Catholic Charities. She eventually had to stop when her Medicare option came through and she was able to start her own private practice. She wanted to continue seeing me out of her apartment in the West Village, but Grandma was already sick and having physical problems by then, and I just couldn't make that trip, so I had to split with her. She was very, very, very disappointed. She wanted to charge me only half—she wanted to do this just for the four clients she wanted to take with her to her private practice—but I just couldn't do it, and she was disappointed. We had had a seven-year relationship, and she didn't want it to end, and she didn't think it *should* end. But I ended it. She did say I was going to be alright.

And I was alright. But I had one incident back then that I'll never forget. She asked me if it would be okay if I met with the staff at Catholic Charities, to do a talk session where they would do all the questioning and I would do all the answering. I said it was okay with me, and I remember when I went to that meeting, there were eight therapists there, and we had a three-hour session—I'll never forget it—and they were throwing all kinds of questions at me. They were all very young. I'll never forget them. This was all for them, for their development. I taught them about that Recovery group that I joined in 1998 or so. I had been doing the therapy and the Recovery group at the same time for years and years. And I was fascinating these young girls, who had never heard of it. I explained that Recovery is a worldwide organization whose goal is to help people with *major* symptoms caused by *minor* incidents. I really taught them something. I said Recovery is free; it's run by a church. Our therapy sessions under normal circumstances are $70 to $100 an hour, but Recovery patients don't pay anything, just like AA meetings that are run out of churches.

CHAPTER 23
How the Neighborhood Changed

We moved into Northridge in the 1950s, and at the time the neighborhood was 100% American—Irish, Italian Christian. Everything was American. The Puerto Ricans started coming into the United States in the early 1950s, but they weren't in Northridge yet. There were only a small number of Jews. When the Civil Rights Act passed around 1965, the Act limited the European immigrants to a much lower number—to only 15%, down from a much higher percentage. You'd have to look up the actual wording of the Act. The other 85% that were allowed to come in would be called "Others," and that's why we are a country of the "Others" now. In the beginning, nothing happened to any of the neighborhoods. Some neighborhoods like Washington Heights, near the George Washington Bridge are about 90% Hispanic. Whole neighborhoods changed over time. I can't say there was a major effect on anyone or anything, but people who didn't like it moved to Forest Hills or Queens, where it was a bit more expensive. The immigrants couldn't afford to go there.

The changes were so gradual over a long period of time—you're talking about 50 years. Take the building here. Originally it was all Jewish. The building was built in 1952. The surrounding neighborhood was all Irish and Italian in private houses. These high rises were going up, and the people really resented it. There was some damage done to businesses too. They didn't want Northridge and then Southridge. The people who lived here were very upset by these co-ops going up. And so our building was 95% Jewish in the mid-1950s and stayed that way until about 1961. The manager literally tried to keep out the "Others"—and he did succeed up until a certain point.

The manager was a single person, not a crew, and his name was Pocher. The guy was amazing because he knew everyone in the three blocks, 1,100 families. When he saw he had a good, stable family, he'd say to the family, "Do you have any brothers or sisters?" And he'd say, "Wouldn't you like for them to come and live here?" He did this with Grandma Rae. He would say, "We could watch for the next opening," and he would do this for all the people—get their families here—to keep the place "pure" or "white," or something, so that there would be no "Others" here.

And he succeeded to a point, up until the early 1960s. But when the schools integrated he couldn't do it anymore, because they broke through. I remember keeping Teddy home for two weeks because Teddy was forced to go to a school in the black neighborhood 15 to 16 blocks away while being denied a bus to get there. He was only 7 or 8 years old when this happened, so it was in the early 1960s.

They would send a whole classroom into the black neighborhood, which was about a mile away from here, and then they'd send a whole class from the black neighborhood into this neighborhood. And I remember, when school started, if you lived more than a mile away from your new school, you were given a bus. We lived 15 or 16 blocks away from the school Teddy was supposed to go to, and we couldn't qualify for a bus. Teddy was only 7 or 8 years old—how was he was supposed to walk sixteen blocks to school every day, across Astoria Boulevard, across major highways? A lot of people kept their kids home until the schools were forced to give them a bus. But up until then, this Pocher guy kept the building "white" and had families bring their extended families in from the Bronx, from Brooklyn, all around, and that's how we ended up there, and Aunt Dottie, and Aunt Mildred. Pocher arranged the whole thing.

When integration started in earnest, a lot of people moved out. The whole thing was planned in the summer months; it was planned privately, and it wasn't told to us until September. They made the announcement two to three weeks before school started, and all the reactions were all over the map, but the parents didn't have time to think things out. They deliberately did that. They said nothing until the very last minute, and it caused a lot of resentment, and a lot of people moved out. My resentment was simply not having a school bus for a 7-year-old kid. But we got the bus finally.

My building changed over the decades. We have 66 apartments here. At least 60 of the 66 apartments were originally Jewish. Today, there are only two Jews left: there's me, and I'm 94, and there's Betty upstairs, and she has to be about 98 years old. And it's the same across all the other buildings in Northridge, which has about seventeen buildings in total—there are only about two Jews in each building. The neighborhood now is at least 75% Hispanic.

The changes happened over a long period of time. But I *love* my neighbors. Grandma and I were closer to our neighbors as we got older than we ever were with the originals in 1954. I have close, close relationships with my neighbors, and I never had that with my Jewish neighbors. As far as I'm concerned, this changeover was a very good thing. I'm old, and I'm not independent anymore, and I have all these neighbors helping me. It just so happens that I'm close to all of them—person to person, people liking each other for whatever reason.

There were plenty of people who were angry about all the store signs being in Spanish—these people are all gone. Whatever Jews or white people are left, they all love it here. They are all happy here, and they understand that they are living in a Spanish neighborhood, and that's that. The Spanish population here is mainly from South and Central America, not so much Mexico and Puerto Rico. It's a warm and friendly community. In fact, the whole world is here. Jackson Heights is known as the most mixed community in the country. If you walk down Roosevelt Avenue where the El train is, and you walk a couple of miles down, every six or seven blocks you're in a different country. If you're in the 70s it's India and Pakistan. If you walk further into the 60s it's the Philippines. In the 50s it's Ireland. That's where your uncle Teddy met his wife Lisa, because he had a bar in Woodside. She came from Dublin and was living in the area. The Irish community there is shrinking, but it was very big at the time, in the late 1900s. The Irish kids were leaving Ireland and coming here because the Irish economy was in trouble. Some of the Irish kids left and went back to Ireland when the economy picked up again, but there are still a lot of Irish mixed in with the Spanish in Woodside.

CHAPTER 24
When the Big Trips with Grandma Ended

The last time I took a trip with Grandma was in 2002 for your cousin Howard's wedding.[6] It was an outdoor wedding on the beach, and we stayed in a hotel. We had to get a clearance from the doctor for her to be able to make this trip, but the doctor said she could go. She had been having health problems, not debilitating, but serious enough to have to make decisions like this. Even though she didn't have the stroke until 2010, she was not 100% anymore after about 2000. She started going downhill.

Instead of these big trips we used to go up from Friday to Monday to Monticello, to the racetrack. We did that a lot in the ensuing years after Howard's wedding, and we loved it. We had good stuff going on locally. She wasn't that sick yet; she just had some nuisance stuff.

We had a wonderful five-year period when we found a restaurant, City Coffee, and we would go there every day for lunch, seven days a week, and we met so many people there over these

---

[6] Howard is the son of my late uncle Stuart, Grandma Rita's brother.

years. This went on from 2004 or 2005 until the stroke finally finished her off in 2010. This was a great time our lives. We developed such a social connection with the men's and women's club in Jackson Heights. I said to them, "I'm not joining any group, but since we're here every week, you can consider us part of the group." This was great for us.

We went to City Coffee every single day, rain or shine. It was a great period, and despite our limitations we came upon this. When it all ended, we stayed in touch with three or four of them up until around 2018.

Eventually City Coffee was sold, and then came the COVID pandemic. (It so happens that the owner of City Coffee died of COVID in 2020.) It was a big loss for Grandma and me when they closed up, because going there was so great for us socially, and we had so many fond memories of the place. They had excellent, excellent Peruvian dishes, or they would make us American dishes, Peruvian style—whatever we wanted. Great memories.

Grandma's Knee

Grandma's knee started bothering her in 2007 or 2008, and that's when all that long walking we used to do came to an end. We were both already close to 80 at that point. I continued the walking, and I did all the shopping on Wednesdays. I'd go to three or four markets, and I must have walked five or six miles every day. My knees were fine then and they're still fine. I'm going to be 95, and my knees are fine. The paddleball guys were not so blessed. Running on concrete is very, very difficult on the knees, whether you're playing basketball or paddleball—the concrete does everybody in. I stopped at 60 but they played another 10 years on that concrete, and they all had knee problems.

But Grandma couldn't take these walks anymore. We still went out to lunch every day. We took a bus to a certain restaurant every day for five years in our eighties. And when we got off the bus, we walked a total of ten blocks, including shopping, etcetera, and then we took a bus back home. But then she needed a cane, and for a while she was able to do it with a cane. For example, that restaurant City Coffee: we went every single day for five years, seven days a week. If there was a snowstorm, they would deliver to us. These were wonderful years.

Grandma had a stroke in 2010 right after surgery on her knee, and she was in rehab for 66 days. I was so excited for her to come home, because I missed her, and because thought it would be so good for her. But it was a disaster. The stroke finished her off. She came home, and she didn't know where anything was. Coming home after that hospital stay, she was not the same anymore. She was permanently damaged. We were going to the neurologist, and he was treating her the best he could. But it was so difficult for her and for me—she didn't want me to leave. I had to ring her once whenever I went out, just to let her know I was okay. And that's how I was able to do the shopping.

She was just finished. From May 2010 to the rest of her life, she was damaged. And she lived until 2022, so we're talking twelve years of this. Toward the end, she was falling a lot, possibly weekly. Most of the time we would pick her up, but twice she was hospitalized, and the last fall was the one that ended up with her not being able to come home.

I did the best I could over those twelve years. These years were brutal. She wasn't a good patient. I remember Teddy being in the house here once, and Grandma was in the little bedroom, and I think she already had the walker, but she saw something she wanted to do, and she didn't take the walker. She just instinctively walked over to whatever it was that she saw, just like she did all her life, and that's when we heard the crash. We heard her go down. There was a lot, a lot of falling, where if she had just held onto her walker or was more aware, she might have avoided it. But she would get an idea in her head, and she'd start walking towards it. And she'd fall. And this was her brain. But this is very common with the elderly, with their frequent, frequent falls. Fortunately I have people here, my neighbors, and they'd come in at 2 in the morning, and they'd pick her up off the floor.

The last time she fell, it was in the bathroom. She fell backwards, and she didn't hit her head this time; she hit her back. She never came back home after that—except for that miracle, that little story that's in the miracle category, which I'm about to tell you.

After the back injury, they sent her home from rehab in the nursing home after she was there for six weeks. They called me up and said she was being discharged, and I assumed she would come back the way she left, but she came back crippled, in a wheelchair, and needing to stay in a wheelchair fulltime. I thought they had patched her up, but in reality, she was being discharged as a wheelchair patient. She came back at about 12 noon, and your mother was there, and I was there, and several other people—an aide, a girl from the bagel store—and they brought Grandma home, and Grandma was a basket case. She was sitting on the recliner, and we're frantic, because your mother wasn't going to be staying overnight, and I remember everyone was frantic trying to find some kind of an aide from the Friday, when she came home, to the coming Monday, when Medicare was going to send a post-discharge evaluation team.

That team is assembled according to an evaluator, who was to come Monday morning. We were not going to have anyone in the house until Monday morning, and we knew right there and then, on that Friday at noon, that without a shadow of a doubt we cannot take care of her, and we don't know what to do. Everyone was making phone calls. And we can't get anybody on the phone.

At 4 o'clock that afternoon, a *miracle* happened—possibly the biggest miracle of my life. I get a phone call from the evaluator who was scheduled to come on Monday. She knows all about Grandma's situation, and she knows the shape Grandma's in. I hadn't spoken to this person in maybe a year, because we had her on a team a year ago for another one of Grandma's episodes.

I pick up the phone, and the voice on the other end of the phone says, "This is Elanna." And I'm stunned, and I'm wondering why she's calling. She said, "I'm calling to tell you to call up the nursing home and tell the nursing home that you're sending her back." And I said, "How can I do that? Why am I doing that? Tell me. I don't even know what's going on." She says to me, "You have 24 hours after discharge to send her back. If you don't send her back by midnight tonight, you're going to have Rita on your hands, and you're going to go through all that crap again from the beginning. You're going to have to call 911. Send. Her. Back." I asked her why she's doing this, and she said, "This is a conscience thing," and she said—she's very religious, and she had to leave early on Friday—that she'd have a big problem on her conscience all weekend if she didn't make this call. She said, "There's no way a 94-year-old man can take care of Rita by himself. I'm doing this partially for you and partially for my conscience. I'm not suggesting. I am *telling* you to do this." And so I'm looking at your mother, and she's looking at me, and she can't figure out that this is not a normal phone call I just got. *This is a miracle.*

This phone call came in and took away the whole problem. I hung up. I called the nursing home, and I said, "We are sending her back. We cannot take care of her." I ended up calling an ambulance, and the ambulance came at 9 at night, and she never came back. That phone call for me personally was in the miracle category. *This was God.*

In fact, this same nurse told me a year ago, she said, "I'm a supervising nurse, and I'm sharing this with you: I really, really like you, and I want to be in contact with you, so this is why I'm telling you this. I've been going to medical school at night. Nobody knows, but I'm one year away from graduating. When I graduate, I'm going to have a medical practice in Queens. And when I graduate, I'm going to be making house calls, and if you're interested, I'd like to make you my first patient." And she did all this with five kids. So I called her up recently and asked her how close she is to graduating. She is sidetracked a little bit right now taking care of her mother, but she's not that far away from graduating.[7] I wanted to know if I was still going to be her first patient. Dr. Babitsky is not that available

---

[7] Elanna is now an MD. She earned her degree sometime in 2023.

anymore, though he's still available 24 hours a day by phone. In person, he's only there about 50% of the time anymore. And I can't go to Rego Park anyway. So, this woman Elanna is 37 years old and I'm keeping in touch with her. She's a very, very religious Orthodox Jewish woman. I'm really interested in taking her up on her offer.

Elvis For a Day

I want to jump back to when Grandma was initially put into the rehab facility, after she fell and hurt her back. She was on the rehab floor, and she's there until she gets discharged. Now, when I went there to visit her, she was not very far away from getting discharged, and I went up there with Janina to see her. I'm getting ready to leave, and I put my coat on, and we say goodbye to Grandma. The doctor walks into this little room—he's got the doctor coat on and his name on his coat, so that's the only reason I knew he was one of the doctors—and somebody comes over to him and exclaims, "Arthur is here!"

So the doctor comes over to me, and he says, "I'm connected to the rehab floor, and I want you to do me a favor. I see you're leaving, but don't leave the building. Take the elevator down to the lobby. Just wait there, because some people from the rehab department want to meet you."

Janina and I went down to the lobby, and we waited for just a couple of minutes when the two side-by-side elevator doors opened at the same time. There were about six of them in one elevator and six of them in the other. And they all start shouting, "There he is!!" And they come running over to me, and Karen, probably the head of the rehab department, says to me, "I'm the one you've been talking to on the phone, and we all couldn't wait to meet you! I want to take a picture with you!" So I said, "With my arm around you?" And she says, "Sure!" And they're taking this picture, and I notice she's got her head on my shoulder for the picture.

Janina and I were trying to figure out what all of this was about, but soon it became very simple: Every minute that Grandma was in that rehab for six to eight weeks, Grandma was talking about me, because I know Grandma. What she said about me exactly, that I don't know, but I know Grandma. But *what* a fuss they made over me. I got a picture with Karen, and Janina took a bunch of pictures too.

When I walked out of that building that day, I said to myself, "Now I know what these stars went through—Elvis Presley, Frank Sinatra—with all these screaming women running after them." I've had a lot of experiences in my life, but this one takes the cake. It was my first visit there, and I found that I had somehow achieved celebrity status.

Grandma's dementia was at full mast by this point, and I had to be the only topic she ever talked about, like a broken record. It was really something. I know the kinds of things she was saying, because when she landed back in that same facility for good, where she was until the day she died, and you and I went to visit her, we both sat there while we witnessed her saying the same sorts of things, over and over and over, while looking at me: "I don't know what I'd do without you ... You're everything ... You're the best thing that ever happened to me ..."

But you know, it didn't take the dementia for her to say things like this. She always said things like this, since the day we met. Just like I said in another part of my story, she used to tell me she thought she died and went to heaven the day she laid eyes on me. I was like a savior to her.

I loved Grandma, and I miss her. But I miss the Grandma who was *well*, not the Grandma who spent the last twelve years of her life battling her stroke and dementia and longing to die. She often expressed wanting to die because she wanted to be "free." These were extremely difficult years for her. When Grandma died, the big emotion I felt was joy, but only because I knew she wasn't suffering anymore. The mourning and the missing—that came later.

CHAPTER 25
This is What It's Like Now

Now let's talk about the difficulty of living this long. I wouldn't call it a blessing living this long. Because I know how I feel, and I know how everyone around me feels, my peers who are living this long. I hear the same stories. Same, same stories all around. Some are handling it better, some are vocal, some are not vocal, but they're all struggling to survive, because of their age, and everything that goes with it.

The most difficult part of this is mental, if I had to pick the *most*. The second one is the loss of mobility: getting up, getting out, and going where you want. I hesitate to even go into a restaurant now. So this is the same as the loss of independence. I had to get my taxes down to Georgia, and I needed someone to go to the post office with me. It's only four short blocks. I said to myself, "Maybe I can make it," and then I realized, "I'd better not try." So these are all losses. What I have going for me, which a lot of people don't, is my social life. I have a large social life. Not face-to-face necessarily anymore, but definitely on the telephone. I don't have a computer, but I can call into my Zoom groups, maybe four or five Zoom groups a week.[8] I'm an active, verbal part of these groups. I'm also very involved in the Life Story Club; some of my stories, like the one about Vic Damone, are featured in their Life Story Library. My special connections there are Stephanie and Lennae.

I'm so lucky that I have the social connection that comes with participation in these groups. But there are a lot of people who are in their 90s, and they are literally, literally alone, and I don't know how they exist being alone like that seven days a week, 24 hours a day. I mean, I feel it on Saturdays and Sundays, when I'm less active. I can't wait for Monday to roll around, and I think about these people who have no one. I have neighbors popping in and out, sometimes five or six in one day. They ring the bell, they come in, and we talk a little, they check on me. I'm fortunate because it's my sociability that makes people come here. I just can't imagine being in my 90s and being seven days a week without anybody.

---

[8] One day in November 2023, a neighbor set up a computer in Grandpa's kitchen and he saw himself on Zoom for the very first time. It was his first experience with the Internet.

My neighbor Anthea comes in and checks on me every single night at 2 in the morning. She glances in. There's enough light from the foyer that she can check on me to make sure I'm still breathing and didn't fall on the floor. If I fell on the floor, I wouldn't be able to use my Life Alert, so she checks on me. My other neighbor Leatrice buys me cases of water bottles and does all sorts of other favors for me. My neighbor Tony checks on me and helps me out, and his wife Esther cuts my hair. And besides these neighbors, I have Yodeli who comes in to do my wash and my food shopping, and now I have Marina, my caregiver, since I'm shut in now. Elanna recommended her to me because she said I'd be better off not dealing with an agency. But these people who have nobody now were more private people to begin with when they were younger, and now they are all alone. I can't imagine it. All they have is those four walls.

[*Why did you decide to turn your stories into a book?*]

My 100% honest answer is this. In passing conversations over my lifetime, I'd say at least 50 times over my lifetime, when we'd be in general conversations, the listener would always say the same thing: you should write a book. And whenever I heard this, I'd say, "What am I going to write a book about?" And I never knew what these people were hearing that I'm not hearing. And this happened as recently as a month ago. Whenever I tell my story, they listen, and they always come back the same way. And I always feel I don't have anything to say that is worthy of becoming a book. But I don't know what they're hearing—not what I'm saying, but what they're *hearing*.

[Did you ever think it's because you're such a good storyteller?]

It's possible that it's because I'm a good storyteller. I'm being told that now in these groups I'm in. I'm in five different groups, and in these groups I tell my stories. There's one group I have, it's a group of caregivers, and I recently went back to this group after Grandma died. The moderator who runs the group, she's from the Alzheimer's Association, and she coined a phrase about certain statements that I have made over the time I've been in the group. She calls them "Arthur-isms." She told me, "When

you were away when Rita passed away, we missed you being here, but what was missing were the Arthur-isms, which are here permanently. They are part of the conversations that go back and forth in this group."
Permanently? I don't even know what they're talking about, but this is what the outside world comes up with.

I don't feel like a storyteller. I feel like I'm just myself, but I have this reputation for being an excellent storyteller, and people do tell me this. I don't hear it, when I go over my life; I don't hear what all these people are hearing and seeing. What sounds amazing to others in the totality of the story, I treat as routine, as normal. This is the way it was. I don't know any other way. Growing up was the way I grew up. I didn't have any other way. I don't know any other way. I'm not so impressed by my own story as they are.

But I hope people will get from this book something like what I got from *Night*. I got so much from that book, but the most important thing I came away with was that even though the parents did so much damage—she had a very similar life to mine—but I felt in reading that story that that mother really, really loved her children. It was the *drugs* that destroyed the parents. The love of the mother for her children was there—*it. was. there.*—versus my story, where there were no drugs, but there was also zero love. Had I ever gotten that author of *Night* on the phone, I would have told her, "I wish I had your mother for my mother, because I could really, really see where your mother cared for you." It was clear to me that the drugs got in the way.

What I think resonates with people is my total story, not the parts. I don't know what it is that makes people feel that it's worthwhile, so I'm doing this for all these people who wanted me to write a book. I don't know what they could possibly get out of my story, but they are clearly getting something out of my stories as I tell them.

I don't know what people are going to think after they read my book, but I hope it will strike them at least in some similar way as *Night* struck me. (Here I am still talking about this book like I read it yesterday.) But every time I tell my story, I feel like I have the same reaction from these same people:

You should write a book.
You should write a book.
You should write a book.

Always the same thing. And so I did. I wonder if something in the writing will hit them the same way that all my storytelling did.

So this is my gift to the "someones" out there— but most especially to the family who came from me, and to all my friends and fans. Maybe when I read this book myself, I'll hear what you're hearing and see what you're seeing.

Acknowledgments

First and foremost, I'd like to thank my Grandpa for taking the time to sit through all of these interviews and answer all my questions, especially when the topics were difficult for you to handle. A lot of wounds were opened up over these months. As the book began to take shape, you were always there to answer my one-off questions. You'd call me plenty of times too, whenever a new story would pop into your head, on the chance that it would make it into the book. I tried to pack in as many stories as I could, and almost all of them are in there.

I'd like to thank my children[9] for their patience with the project. It's closing in on almost a year now, and you sacrificed plenty of "Mommy time" to let me take these calls and develop the text for the book. You must have sensed the importance of this project, and you helped make it happen by giving me the space to do it. I hope you treasure this book and pass it down to your children and grandchildren as a legacy. This book is *not* the stuff of Hallmark cards, but I know you'd rather keep things real, and that's what I did.

---

[9] James, David (Dave), Benjamin, Gioia, Michael Jr. (Mikey), and Milo.

I can't thank my husband, Mike DellaVecchia, fellow writer and editor, enough for his involvement with the project. He not only proofread the book but also made invaluable editorial/developmental suggestions for additional interviews with Grandpa, ones that were needed to tie certain names or threads together. Without your experience as a writer and journalist, and without your excellent sense of narrative and perspective-taking, this book would not have turned out as well as it did. You also took my vision for a cover design and put it into motion, adding your own design touches and using your extensive graphic design skills to create a cover that I fell in love with.

I owe my mother Sharon all my love and thanks for bringing me into this world and doing the best she could, despite all odds and obstacles. I'm here today because of the sacrifices you made. The old pictures of us, the ones I showed you and included in the book, took my breath away.

Of course I can't end this without thanking God for my life, my family, the pains, and the joys.

And we know that all things work together for good to them that love God, to them who are the called according to his purpose. – Romans 8:28

www.ingramcontent.com/pod-product-compliance
Lightning Source LLC
Chambersburg PA
CBHW050325010526
44119CB00003B/104